First published 1994
© Mike Mansley

Mike Mansley has asserted his rights under the Copyright, Designs and Patents Act 1988, to be identified as the author of this work.

Published by Michael J Mansley
44 Dan-y-graig Avenue
Porthcawl, Mid Glamorgan CF36 5AA, United Kingdom

First printed in the United Kingdom in 1994 by

Harris Printers
18 Mary Street, Porthcawl, Mid Glamorgan CF36 3YA

A CIP catalogue record of this book is available from the British Library

ISBN 0 9523152 0 3

All rights reserved

No part of this book may be reproduced, stored in a retrieval system or transmitted in any form or by any means, electronic, mechanical, photocopying, recording or otherwise, without the written permission of Michael J Mansley.

CONTENTS

INDEX		*i - iii*
CHAPTER ONE -	THE CIVILIANS	*22*
CHAPTER TWO -	THE HOME GUARD	*23 - 30*
CHAPTER THREE -	THE ROYAL OBSERVER CORPS	*31 - 36*
CHAPTER FOUR -	THE BRITISH ARMY	*37 - 46*
CHAPTER FIVE -	RAF STORMY DOWN	*47 - 72*
CHAPTER SIX -	AIR SEA RESCUE	*73 - 82*
CHAPTER SEVEN -	THE DUTCH	*83 - 91*
CHAPTER EIGHT -	THE AMERICANS	*92 - 108*
INDEX		*109 - 111*

INTRODUCTION

In 1992 I undertook the task of writing the historical section of the Porthcawl Town Guide. When the first draft was completed, the then Mayor, Councillor Madeline Moon, pointed out that there was very little in it that described life in the town during the war years of 1939-45 and I tried to remedy this to some extent by including a passage about that period in the final version of the Guide.

I soon realised the wealth of information that was hidden away in memories and archives and when the Town Guide was completed I set about researching as much as it was possible to find about the wartime period. Porthcawl is a small coastal town, looking out across the Bristol Channel to the North Devon coast. During the war it welcomed thousands of British, French, Dutch, Canadian, Polish and American servicemen and women, who were accommodated in hotels, guest houses, nissen huts and tents and who trained at the nearby RAF airfield or amongst the sand-dunes and on the beaches. The civilian population carried on with their daily lives and accepted the blackout, food shortages and presence of large numbers of very fit young men as the necessary ingredients of winning the war.

The story of the military "invasion" of Porthcawl would almost certainly apply to other small towns throughout Southern Britain, where the indigenous population was swamped by the armed services, particularly during the build up to D-Day. However, in addition to the presence in the town of thousands of British and Allied servicemen and women, Porthcawl also enjoyed the added experience of a large RAF training station on the outskirts of the town and an Air Sea Rescue Base in the harbour.

I have spoken to and exchanged correspondence with a considerable number of civilians and service veterans and I am most grateful to all of them for their help. Listing those who have recalled the past is very dangerous because inevitably someone will be missed and if this is the case here, please accept my apologies. Amongst those who have helped me are:-

Alexander C Allen (USA), Lt. Col Ashwood & Major R P Smith (South Wales Borderers & Monmouthshire Regimental Museum), Roger E Athans (USA), Mrs Anna Azoulay (Royal Netherlands Embassy), Betty Austin, Ken Baker, Kenneth

Carr, Ben Clarke, Tony Comley, Walter Cooper, Ray Cottrell, John David, T.A. Davies, Joe Dzwonkowski (USA), Fred DeMary (USA), Paul B Ellis Jr. (USA), Mike Flynn, Harry Grant, H. Hertel (Holland), Bert Hayward, Henk J Jansen (Holland), J. Barry Jones, D Morgan Joseph, Bernard LaDuke (USA), Dale F Means (Society of American Military Engineers), Carl V Moore (USA), Mr Morgan Marks, Doreen Owen, Gwyn Petty, Dennis Purchase, John Rippin, Hans Sonnemans (Holland), J. de Vries (Holland), Jack de Waal (Holland), L. Wassen (Holland), Colin Walker, W.E. White, John Williams (RNLI), Jack Winchester, Nancy Wornum and her late husband, Ralph.

The wartime editions of the "Glamorgan Gazette" were an invaluable source of information and I have obtained information from the Public Record Office files Air 28/724, 29/448, 29/477, 29/588, 29/591, 29/592/, 29/634, 29/1574, 29/2264 and 29/ 2573. Photographs of the types of aircraft that flew from Stormy Down are reproduced with the kind permission of the Royal Air Force Museum, Hendon. Parts of the account of the 15th Battalion, the Welch Regiment, were taken from Chapter X111 of "The History of the Welch Regiment 1919-1951" by kind permission of the Trustees of the Welch Regiment Museum. The information about the 4th Monmouthshire Battalion of the South Wales Borderers was kindly supplied by the Curator of the Regimental Museum, Brecon. The history of the Royal Observer Corps was supplied by the headquarters of that organisation at Bentley Priory, Stanmore and permission to use the 1952 photograph of the Observation Post at Locks Lane was kindly given by the Home Office. I am grateful to the Ministry of Defence for granting me permission to publish the 1946 aerial photograph of RAF Stormy Down. Information and photographs about the Dutch Army were supplied by the History and Documentation Foundation of the Royal Netherlands 'Prinses Irene' Brigade, Best; the Netherlands Embassy in London and by Mr Hans Sonnemans of the Garde Regiment Fusiliers Prinses Irene, Eindhoven.

A bibliography for the 107th Field Artillery Battalion (U.S. 28th Infantry Division) and the 75th Infantry Division was supplied by the U. S. Army Centre of Military History, Washington D.C. Finally I would like to thank the Porthcawl Museum & Historical Society for many of the photographs that appear in this book.

For a much more detailed account of RAF Stormy Down and the Air Sea Rescue

Unit than I have provided I strongly recommend Ray Cottrell's unpublished document "Semper Alacer", a copy of which is held in the Porthcawl Public Library. I have tried to provide as much information as possible about the day to day activities of the townspeople and of the many military and civilian emergency service units that were present in Porthcawl during the war. In some cases, such as with RAF Stormy Down and the Air Sea Rescue Unit, the amount of available information might justify a book itself. In other cases I have been able to offer all the information that I have unearthed. Regrettably, in the final category come those services about which no records appear to exist or veterans can be traced to tell their stories. In this latter category are included the Auxiliary and National Fire Services, the Special Police and Glamorgan Constabulary and the search light and anti-aircraft batteries. I apologise for this omission but I hope that it will provide a helpful historical record of Porthcawl's contribution to the defeat of Hitler.

Mike Mansley
Porthcawl   May 1994.

CHAPTER ONE

THE CIVILIANS

Prime Minister Neville Chamberlain's announcement on September 3, 1939, that "we are now at war with Germany" was received throughout the country with a mixture of foreboding, of relief that the waiting was over and with an enthusiasm to become involved with the fight to defend the homeland from invasion by the Nazi hordes. In Porthcawl, a small Welsh coastal town overlooking the Bristol Channel, the announcement generated considerable concern about the lack of provision of air-raid shelters. Porthcawl Urban District Council debated the problem, which had been highlighted by Miss Lucy Brogden, daughter of James Brogden, who had been the driving force behind the construction of the harbour and of Porthcawl town in the 19th Century. Miss Brogden told the Council that a number of people had come from London to escape the air-raids, but had returned once they had learned that there were no air-raid shelters in the town. The Councillors were advised that Porthcawl only ranked as a category "B" in the priority for provision of public shelters, whilst Port Talbot was a category "A".

This did not satisfy at least one of the Councillors. "The only thing we can hope" said Councillor J.T. Lewis "is that there will never be an air-raid on Porthcawl. If there is someone will have to answer for it!" This warning appears to have reached the Reich, because no bombs fell on Porthcawl throughout the war, although the nearby Stormy Down R.A.F Station was attacked.

Concern was also expressed that no equipment had arrived for the four men who had been appointed as a Rescue Squad and that although a Central Clearing Station had been set up in the Lesser Hall (now the Jubilee Room) beneath the Grand Pavilion, the eight spray baths which should have been provided for men and women (segregated) had not arrived.

The Urban District Council was worried about where the responsibility lay for cleaning the Lesser Hall, beneath the Grand Pavilion (and now called the "Jubilee Room"), it was used at night by the A.R.P. and by women ambulance drivers of the Red Cross, but no one had accepted responsibility for cleaning up the mess which they apparently left. The Council did not think that the costs of cleaning should fall to the rates.

There was a problem regarding the effectiveness of the air-raid siren. This could be heard within the town itself, but the residents of Newton and Nottage complained that they could only hear it if the wind was blowing in the right direction. In August, 1940, 70 residents of Locks Common petitioned the Council because they could not hear it.

The Air Raid Precaution (A.R.P) organisation was responsible for organising the arrangements for enforcing blackouts and dealing with the effects of air-raids. There was considerable controversy about the fact that some A.R.P. Wardens were being paid whilst others were not. Mr Conway Jenkins, then Senior Warden of Porthcawl A.R.P., wrote to the "Glamorgan Gazette" in October, 1939, about the gossip that he and his fellow wardens were being paid for their services. He explained that at least three wardens were patrolling the town and receiving payment "but they have not passed an examination nor received a badge and certificate which others had done in 1938". He had spoken to one of the three and he had claimed that he hadn't wanted the job - it had been forced on him! Mr Jenkins commented on the confused state of affairs where forced men were being paid and volunteers were not. He gave an assurance, however, that "when the sirens sounded, the volunteers would be there".

Mr Walter Cooper of West Road, Nottage, became a warden in 1938 and qualified for a badge and certificate. He recalled that the training was in the Grand Pavilion, and was mainly concerned with the effects of a gas attack. When war was declared unqualified local businessmen were put in charge of the A.R.P., to the dismay of those who had passed their examinations, and some odd instructions were issued. One of these was that the wardens' equipment (tin hat and gas mask) must be kept in a central point in the town. This meant that when the alarm sounded Mr Cooper had to cycle to South Road, collect his tin hat and gas mask and return to his patrol area in Nottage!
Mr Cooper remembered the air attacks on Swansea which took place over three consecutive nights; "The German aircraft were circling the area above Porthcawl and Pyle, preparing to dive on Swansea. The few anti-aircraft guns were doing all they could and shrapnel was falling all around. Swansea looked like a giant sea of flame. My wife and I looked out of our bedroom window at the awful sight and watched a German bomber over Swansea Bay; it was hit and exploded in mid-air."

Another resident, Mr Jim Lock, recalled the sight of an Air-Raid Warden, fully equipped in a white helmet, riding his bicycle around the street as the siren wailed and urging the householders to take cover amongst the rocks below Locks Common.

The matter of payment to the auxiliary services also gave concern to the regular Fire Service. In September 1939 the Council considered complaints that volunteer firemen were being paid £3 per week whilst the regular firemen were working 50-60 hours without any extra payment. The Chairman of the Council, Dr Chalke delivered the rebuke that "we find ourselves in one of the most terrible crises the country has ever known. I think it is a test of our patriotism".

Those Porthcawl residents who read the "Glamorgan Gazette" were surprised to read in October, 1939, that the famous woman aviator, Amy Johnson, had been in trouble with the police a few miles outside the town. Amy, who had been born in 1903, became the nation's heroine when she flew solo to Australia in 1930, to Tokyo in 1932 and to and from the Cape of Good Hope in 1936. A popular song was written about her and in 1939 she was actively engaged as a civilian in wartime flying duties and was based in Cardiff (possibly St. Athan). On September 11, 1939, a Police Sergeant, a Constable and an A.R.P. Warden were on duty on the A48 at St. Nicholas when two cars came towards them with their headlights blazing, which was, of course, strictly forbidden. The cars were stopped and the driver of the first car was warned, but he was not dealt with quickly enough for the following driver who shouted out "How much **** longer are you going to keep me here?" This turned out to be Amy Johnson, who was asked to produce her driver's license. "I'm **** if I will" said Amy and she accelerated away, with P.C. Coombes on the footboard of the 30hp car, reaching through the side window and trying to turn off the ignition. His hand was pierced by Amy's fingernails but the car was brought to a stop and the aviator was dragged out of it. Amy was charged with numerous offences (including not having a driver's license) and confessed to six previous motoring convictions. She was fined a total of £6.11.6 (£6.57 1/2p).
Sadly Amy Johnson died on 5 January 1941. Whilst ferrying a military aircraft for the Air Transport Auxiliary, she took off in dense fog from an airfield in South-East England and the plane developed engine trouble. She baled out over the Thames Estuary and died in the icy water before help could reach her. A Royal Navy captain who dived in to try to save her also died.

Showing too much light was a problem experienced by motorists and householders alike. Many motorists were prosecuted for failing to comply with the regulations as were those who were responsible for blackout precautions in private and public buildings. The landlord of the "Jolly Sailor" was fined £1.2.6d (1.12 1/2p) for showing a light directly up into the sky and a "Glamorgan Gazette" columnist reported that he was enjoying an evening in Porthcawl in the company of an R.A.F. serviceman when a light was seen breaking the otherwise complete blackness shrouding the town. On investigation they found that the light was coming from the Council Offices in South Road and the R.A.F. serviceman, no doubt concerned that this might lead the Dorniers to R.A.F. Stormy Down, raced up the stairs and tore the offending lighting fitting from the ceiling!

Motorists were also prosecuted for not showing any lights at all because the regulations required that parked vehicles were required to display parking lights. The amount of light which could be exposed caused some confusion and many motorists found themselves in trouble because their parking lights were too bright. In one case the residents in a street where a number of cars were parked at night became fearful that the lights would attract German bombers and called on the drivers to go away. The regulations for motor cars required headlamps to be hooded, with a slit for light not more than 3/8" wide. No light was to be visible from more than 25 feet away and was not to be higher than eye level. Rear lights, also, had to be screened.

There was considerable heart-searching amongst the Porthcawl Urban District Councillors about the times of opening on Sundays of the town's cinemas. The country might have been fighting for its freedom but there was deep concern that cinemas were opening as early as 7p.m. on a Sunday, instead of the accepted 8 p.m. Mr William Beynon then caused some confusion by applying for a license to open his two cinemas, the Coliseum (now "Lo-Cost") and Casino (now the burnt out site of the Stoneleigh Club) on a Sunday, in spite of the fact that he had been opening on Sundays for some years without applying for a license. After heated discussion the license was granted. It is, perhaps, worth mentioning that cinemas in Port Talbot and Bridgend were not allowed to open on Sundays at all.

The people of Porthcawl were enthusiastically helping the large number of troops who were coming into the town. In June 1940, 2000 exhausted survivors of the Dunkirk rescue operation arrived and were billeted in various houses, including

Taken in 1953, John Street looking essentially the same as it did during the war. Note the frontages of Woolworths and the Porthcawl Hotel.

Ocean View and also the Rest. In the daytime they stretched out on the Esplanade and many residents gave them tea and cakes. Mr Jim Lock recalled that his mother set up a small canteen for the survivors in her house at 43 West Drive and that she continued this service on throughout the war for the British and American servicemen. The front room was converted into a shop and teas and refreshments were served through a side window, an adjacent garage providing shelter.

Mrs Wornum of Victoria Avenue remembers her mother, Mrs M. Linton Wilson, working with the Womens Voluntary Service (W.V.S.), running a Meals on Wheels service which started in the kitchen of the Highfield Chapel and which cooked up to 30 meals every day. Mrs Wilson also wove camouflage netting for the Army in a wooden shack behind Woolworth's and also darned socks and did needlework repairs for the soldiers.

In June 1940 Porthcawl experienced its first large scale influx of evacuees. One little girl enquired on her arrival "Can you speak English here?" and the confirmation that the residents could (and did) presumably reassured the remaining 342 children and 61 adults, who were welcomed by the Chairman of the Porthcawl Council, Dr Chalke, and helped to their new homes by members of the St. John's Ambulance Brigade, Red Cross and British Legion. Children came from many parts of England, including 470 from Chatham and Rochester in Kent and others from Birmingham. In 1944 Porthcawl Town Council received a letter from Birmingham City Council expressing its "high appreciation of and grateful thanks for the excellent services rendered by Porthcawl to the children evacuated from Birmingham".

Although loutish behaviour by some of the younger members of our society is considered to be a modern phenomenon, it is interesting to read that on August Bank Holiday, 1940, groups of "young hooligans", wearing paper hats, were reported to have jeered at soldiers and played football on the Esplanade Promenade, to the annoyance of passers-by. The reporter states that he personally saw two children knocked over by these hooligans. It is probable, however, that the exuberance of these young men would soon have been directed towards fighting Hitler, a remedy that is no longer available.

The Grand Pavilion was playing a leading role in the uplifting of public morale. The Council received a letter congratulating it on the nightly concerts and dances

The Esplanade Promenade, just after the war, with the Sea Bank Hotel, "Home" to many of the servicemen who were stationed in Porthcawl, and the Grand Pavilion.

Porthcawl Museum

it had organised and it was reported that takings had increased by £2320 above previous years. As many as 800 people attended each of the Sunday evening concerts and a total of 15,000 people had attended the various functions since the blackout began in 1939. In October 1940 Dame Sybil Thorndike and the Old Vic Company was given a Civic Reception and gave performances of "Macbeth" on two nights to a packed Grand Pavilion.

On one Sunday in December, 1940, "Porthcawl's Big Night" in the Pavilion attracted an audience of more than 1000 - a surprisingly high attendance since there were only 2400 houses in the town at that time. The evening started with community singing, accompanied by an electric organ, and this was followed by an address by Mr William Courtney, "an eminent authority on air warfare". The audience was then entertained by Mr Towyn Harries, "the well known tenor" and by Madame Renie White, described as a nationalist winner and gold medallist, assisted by the boy soprano, David Walford Jones. The evening was "a real treat for those who wanted to forget their worries for one night".

As Porthcawl entered 1941 preparations began to deal with the threat of incendiary bombs. The Council agreed to provide sand for every house "as a measure against any forthcoming fire blitz", and called for volunteers to form fire parties. The Council also announced that it had joined in the race to form units of the then Air Cadet Corps (later to be known as the "Air Training Corps"). Porthcawl and Newport were the first local authorities in Wales to sponsor units and on 23 May 1941 it was confirmed that a Commanding Officer had been appointed and that volunteers were joining the new squadron.

Porthcawl's residents were being urged to eat more carrots, oatmeal and potatoes. Stocks of the latter throughout the country were said to be so high that unless more were eaten they would have to be fed to the livestock. Carrot jam was recommended as also were carrot tarts and flans ("so surprisingly good both to look at and to eat that every housewife should try them on her husband"!)

In February, 1941, the townspeople were told "How Britain will smash a Nazi invasion".

"Some enemy might succeed in landing. By air and sea they might descend upon selected spots in Great Britain. There might be many thousands of them, perhaps many tens of thousands. Could they take possession of the country and extort a surrender? Whatever may have been the position six months ago, every qualified authority is ready to answer an emphatic "No!" Provided only that the British people keep their heads and act with the same calm courage and prompt energy which they have shown in dealing with air attack, the invasion would certainly be crushed. Every enemy soldier would be killed or captured. Britain today is alert and armed. She has strong coast defenses. She has a great army at home trained and equipped for sudden ruthless action. She has a Home Guard of nearly two millions whose units have reached a most creditable standard of efficiency. Fighting in the countryside whose every feature they have known for years they would deprive an invader of all freedom of movement and hand him over crippled for the deathblow. The enemy would encounter the soul and spirit of a united free people - and that would bring them to ultimate and complete defeat".

Special Constable R.P.T. Deere, a prominent Estate Agent at that time and from 1947 an Urban District Councillor and later Chairman of the Council, might have raised an eyebrow about the reference to the "strong coast defenses". His duties included patrolling the beach at Newton. Long after the war ended he told his son, David, that "there was only one gun shared between six men and no-one knew how to fire it!"

Nevertheless, duly encouraged by this assurance of the nation's invincibility, Porthcawl's civilians organised a "War Weapons Week" between 29 March and 5 April, 1941, with the target of raising £25,000, an ambitious sum since, as has previously been mentioned, there were only 2400 houses in the Urban District at that time. The Week was launched by Mr W.J. Brown, General Secretary of the Civil Service Clerical Association, and Mr Jack Jones, the Welsh author and dramatist and the first event was a football match between the Army & the R.A.F. A whist and bridge drive was held in the Casino Ballroom and a Sale of Work took place in the Girl Guides' hut. The Casino ballroom was also the venue for a "Grand Dance".
These and other activities and donations from some of Porthcawl's residents raised a total of £76,709, three times the target and a quite incredible amount when converted into today's value of £2,408,662! (Based on the 1938 Retail Prices Index. No data is available for the R.P.I. in the war years).

The impact of the war was beginning to touch some of Porthcawl's families. In

April, 1941, it was announced that Sub Lt. Evan David, R.N. of the Naval Air Arm and the son of Mr & Mrs John David of Eastnor House, who had been killed in action in February, had been awarded the D.F.C. He had been serving with the R.A.F. and was at that time the third Porthcawl serviceman to receive the award. He was an old boy of St. John's School, Newton. The other two who received D.F.C's were Pilot Officer Peter Price and Pilot Officer Kenneth Illingworth Hamill, also an old boy of St. John's, whose home was at "Antrim" in South Place. Kenneth Hamill had been captain of St. John's Football and Cricket Elevens in 1934 and joined the R.A.F. in 1939. He was awarded a DFC in July 1940, was promoted to F/Lt in 1941 and Squadron Leader in 1942. In 1943 it was announced that Squadron Leader Hamill had been killed in air operations in India at the age of 25. Although his name appears on the town's war memorial, for some reason it is as Sqd Ldr Kenneth Illingworth. In 1945 another St. John's old boy, Peter Lewis, was awarded the DFC.

Porthcawl Urban District Council's blackout problems surfaced again in April, when the Council's Clerk was in the dock answering a charge of allowing a light to be shown from the landing and from two uncovered windows in South Road Council Offices. The Clerk explained that the gas light which illuminated a dark staircase and not been turned off when the staff left the building. The magistrate was most unsympathetic - "I noticed it was stated in the press recently that members of your Council were talking about the blackout in Porthcawl being disgraceful and asking 'Where are the police?' Now this is what happens!" The Council was fined £2 and the Clerk and other Council Officers suffered further unsympathetic criticism from the Councillors at the next Council meeting.

The great Ambulance debate occupied a great deal of attention in 1941. An "ambulance car" had been bought by public subscription mainly for transporting sick residents to and from Bridgend General Hospital, there being no official ambulance available in the town. Management of the ambulance was the responsibility of a committee, which included members of the Ratepayers' Association, but serious problems arose in organising its availability and in meeting its running costs. The policy was that those who could afford to pay for using the facility should make a contribution, but unfortunately few were prepared to do so. Difficulty was also experienced in obtaining the ambulance and one Councillor complained that it had been necessary for him to make several telephone calls before he could arrange transport for a sick resident.

The "Ambulance Committee" was extremely unhappy about the problems of running the ambulance and a deputation attended a Town Council meeting and offered the vehicle to the Council. An argument subsequently developed between the Councillors over whether the deputation was authorised to make the offer. In desperation, the Ambulance Committee then offered the vehicle to the Ratepayers Association, without success. However, finally, the Urban District Council accepted the ambulance car - and set up a committee of seven to manage its use.

The Committee set about organising a more effective financing discipline. Those using the ambulance were charged 9d per mile, with a minimum charge of 5/ - (25p), Any person who was unable to meet the cost could make an application to be excused the charge "without enquiries being made into the pecuniary circumstances of the applicant".

In June 1941 the Council became concerned about the absence of any volunteers for fire-watching duties from those with business premises in John Street and that consideration would have to be given to applying for compulsory powers of registration. It was pointed out, however, that a number of local men were in the Forces or were serving in the Observer Corps, Special Police, ARP and Auxiliary Fire Service. Several Councillors spoke of the possibility of recruiting ladies as "fire watchers" and it was noted that the Head Warden had organised a scheme by which a number of ladies would take charge of the stirrup pumps should the need arise. Confidence was expressed that "the women of the town would respond if an appeal was made to them".

Difficulties in finding photographs taken during wartime Porthcawl are possibly explained by the experience of a schoolteacher from Mountain Ash on a day trip to Porthcawl in June 1941. He took one photograph and was pounced upon and arrested by a Police Constable. He later appeared before the local magistrates, who fortunately accepted his plea that the offense had been carried out innocently and charged him twenty five shillings costs (£1.12 1/2p).

Rationing and food shortages were by now affecting most residents and shopping became a major worry to housewives, particularly in trying to be at the shops when items which were in short supply became available. In August, 1941, it was reported that the Council had received complaints that Porthcawl's traders were opening early and selling to day-trippers and visitors. "By doing so, residents are deprived of numerous articles of food as it is not possible for those who have families to attend to in the morning or who have visitors to cater for, to indulge in early morning expeditions".

It was pointed out that in winter local tradesmen were dependent on the ratepayers of Porthcawl for their livelihood and that in fairness the residents should get preferential treatment over the visitors in summer. The Council recognised that traders made their living by catering to visitors and that it could not be expected that they would make no provision for visitors and trippers. It was decided to write to the Chamber of Trade to ask that they consider not selling goods to visitors before 3p.m. This would "avoid the problem of day trippers arriving early, scouring the town and departing laden with things that local people have to do without".

The Mother Abbess and four nuns from St. Clare's Convent, Newton, found themselves in the magistrates' court in September, 1941. It was a requirement that all letters to Ireland, both North and South, should be examined by the Postal Censor, under the Control of Communications Order, 1941. Nuns travelling on holiday to Northern Ireland sometimes carried letters from others in the convent to their friends and relations and unfortunately this practice was referred to in a letter that was intercepted by the censors and which somewhat tactlessly referred to their inquisitive nature; "you may be sure that there are some busy-bodies there; there are lots of Lurgan girls in the censorship office in Belfast". A fine of £1 and costs of £1.15/ - were imposed. There is no report of the reaction of the Lurgan girls to this sentence!

The year 1941 ended with a free cinema show for the children on Christmas Day morning and on New Years' Day. A pantomime was organised for December 20 and special entertainment was provided for the evacuees.

The removal of railings from private and public properties began in 1942 in order to satisfy the tremendous demands of the war industry. It was explained that the railings which had enclosed Hyde Park in London, amounting to 450 tons, had been converted into anti-aircraft guns and that those removed from the front gardens of Porthcawl's residents would be similarly used. There were complaints, however, about the damage caused during the removal and of the problems of cattle straying into gardens. One casualty was the beautifully maintained garden opposite to where the Sandpiper Pub now stands. This was protected by the railings and by a gate that was locked at night. It soon became unkempt and it is now an uninteresting stretch of often litter strewn grass.

Porthcawl saw the opening of its "British Restaurant" in July, 1942. These restaurants were opening up all over the country and provided well cooked meals at very economic prices, which helped to supplement the very frugal ration allowance. There had been public demand for one in Porthcawl for some time and there was great enthusiasm when the British Restaurant was opened in the premises now occupied by "The Clock Shop" by the Chief Divisional Food Officer, Sir Thomas G Jones, KBE. In his speech he disclosed that the Chairman of the Council had come to Porthcawl to die. He attributed his full recovery to regularly drinking the water from the well at Newton.

The Restaurant proved to be extremely popular and arrangements had to be made to control the queues waiting outside. Later in the year it was agreed that teas and suppers should also be served, partly to make up for the loss of visitors who had patronised the Restaurant during the summer.

In August, 1942, it was reported that the shelters in the Grand Pavilion were being regularly used for informal evening concerts. Hundreds of visitors were gathering to listen to and join in the signing of Welsh hymns and to impromptu solos given by members of the audience. At one of these concerts the audience was surprised to learn that the Master of Ceremonies was a Londoner "but that inspite of this he pronounced the names of the Welsh hymns with ease".

The Council had a fierce debate in December 1942 over a request by the Operatic Society to hire the Grand Pavilion for three nights. Unfortunately this would have included the Wednesday and Wednesday night was Dance Night. "God help mankind if it is going to look for emancipation from dancing" thundered one councillor. "There are more things in life than the dance floor". The councillors emphasised that they "were not against the young having their fling". Another was "amazed when some of the leading lights in this town use the best building in Porthcawl for the sake of dancing and making money".
In the end "The Student Prince" won the day and the Wednesday Dance was cancelled.

In March 1943 Porthcawl's residents once again dug deep down into their pockets and purses in support of "Wings for Victory Week". It was reported that the Week began with "the finest parade the town has ever seen", with contingents of the armed forces, together with several bands, including one consisting entirely of W.A.A.Fs (Womens' Auxiliary Air Force). A Defiant fighter aircraft was parked in Griffin Park, with a rubber dinghy beside it to receive donations. An indicator outside the Casino (later the Stoneleigh Club and now demolished) registered the total amount collected and this was changed daily at noon. A huge model plane was suspended above the Grand Pavilion, with an appropriate slogan beneath. A streamer across John Street reminded shoppers that it was "Wings for Victory" Week and there was a large display of model aeroplanes and "other interesting exhibits" in the Casino.

At the rear of the Grand Pavilion a 500 lb bomb casing was positioned. People were invited to buy savings stamps and plaster them on the bomb, which would later be filled with High Explosive and dropped on Germany.

At the end of the Week a total of £80,000 had been raised, equivalent to £1.5 million at 1992 prices. This was sufficient to pay for four Mosquito bombers and it included a donation of £1500 from Porthcawl Senior School. Nottage Council School did even better and raised £2000. Porthcawl Urban District Council was presented with a plaque which was attached to the wall in the Pavilion. When renovations were being carried out to the Pavilion in recent years, Mr John David spotted the plaque and another presented for "Salute the Soldier" Week in 1944 in a skip, ready for collection and disposal at the local tip. They were rescued and can now be seen in the Porthcawl Museum.

Amazingly almost as much was raised from Porthcawl's townspeople in May, 1943, when it held a "Warship Week". A target of £50,000 was set and £67,000 was achieved, equivalent now to £1,262,000. A town plaque was presented to Captain Pritchard of the Royal Navy and this was fixed on to MTB 84. An Admiralty plaque was presented to Porthcawl U.D.C. and this can been seen in the Porthcawl Museum.

The part played by the Grand Pavilion in maintaining a high level of morale through the darkest days of the war is shown by the figures released by Porthcawl Urban District Council in April 1943. During 1942 to 1943, it had been used for

Porthcawl Museum

"Wings for Victory" parade, 27th March 1943.

27 private functions. A total of 133,664 people had paid to attend dances, with 85,476 attending as balcony spectators. 37,599 had supported the free Thursday concerts, of which there had been 182 with a total attendance of 170,000 since September 1939.

In April 1944 Porthcawl was once again raising funds for the war effort. "Salute the Soldier Week" was launched with a target of £70,000. The newspapers urged support of the campaign with an advertisement showing a soldier, his right arm bearing three stripes and an A.T.S. girl with two stripes, drinking tea in a railway station buffet, kitbags beside them. Headed "The Corporal & the Sarge", the advertisement read:

> *They only meet to lose again*
> *They only meet to part*
> *They've little time to linger*
> *With the language of the heart*
> *She to her radio station*
> *He for the road to Rome*
> *There's much to do and far to go*
> *Before they both come home.*
> *And he must march full many a mile*
> *And fight through change and charge*
> *Ere he promotes his Corporal*
> *And makes her Mrs Sarge.*

Although this would now evoke cries of derision, it reflects the emotions of those who were caught up in a bloody war, who might be parted for years. Nowadays it would be dismissed as mawkish sentimentality but in 1944 everyone could sympathise with the sentiments expressed and there were many sons of Porthcawl's townspeople who were on the road to Rome - and to many other towns occupied by the enemy.

Sentimental or not it certainly encouraged Porthcawl's residents to support "Salute the Soldier Week". In one week £107,290 was raised, equivalent to £2,021,492 at 1992 prices! Porthcawl took the County Championship flag from Penarth as a result of this magnificent effort.

Whilst the Sergeant was fighting his way to Rome, Porthcawl Council was debating whether the action of police who had moved in to stop a crowd from singing on the seafront was justified. Councillor Burnell pointed out that singing was prohibited within 100 yards of an inhabited house if there was an objection. Other councillors complained that the noise of young people (including girls) singing filthy songs was keeping residents awake at night. Dr Chalke believed that "we should encourage anything in the nature of hymn or glee singing provided it is dignified and fervent".
The Council decided to seek permission for community singing and to ask the police to control "unruly singing".

Thoughts were already turning to Victory and to the return of the soldiers from abroad. A "Welcome Home Troops Fund" was established in 1944, with a target of raising £10,000 by 1945. Weekly dances were organised in the Grand Pavilion but the Council rejected an appeal for hire charges to be waived on the grounds that it would costs the ratepayers £6000 in lost revenue.

One soldier who returned had suffered nearly five years imprisonment as a prisoner of war. Driver Glyndwr Thomas of the Royal Army Service Corps, whose home was in Fenton Place, had joined the services in 1939 and had been captured by the Germans at St. Valery in France in June 1940. He revealed the hardships under which the men had suffered at the prisoner of war camp in Marienburg, East Prussia.. "The first two years were the hardest. For the first eight or nine months we existed on German rations consisting of one loaf of bread per day divided amongst five men, one small pat of margarine, one pint of barley and potato soup and one pint of ersatz (imitation) coffee per man, with no milk or sugar. Then the Red Cross parcels arrived as a Godsend and we can never thank the Red Cross enough for the wonderful work they have done". Porthcawl's Red Cross shop had raised money throughout the war and when it closed in July 1945 it had raised a record total throughout the country of £7572 (equivalent to £143,000 at today's prices).

The Grand Pavilion continued to be the main centre of entertainment. In April, 1945, a cast of 75 performed "The Kingdom of God" in the Grand Pavilion, in aid of the "Welcome Home Troops" fund; the Pavilion was filled to capacity the following Sunday night for a concert given by the Tonyrefail & Ely Valley Male Voice Choir. In the same month an Old English Dance (a "special Easter treat for the older people") was provided in the Pavilion and the "Welcome Home Fund" Committee organised "Cinderella", "an excellent pantomime that played to a packed house". In May there was an R.A.F. Dance and the Cardiff National Fire Service Drama Company performed "Tons of Money" to packed houses on two nights. This drama company was popular with Porthcawl's residents; it had previously performed "A Murder Has Been Arranged" and "Charley's Aunt".

R.A.F. personnel presented a revue "Slipstream" on 17 May, and this was followed by the usual Thursday night competition for the troops. Private Yerley (soloist) won first prize, Private Cropper (Ventriloquist) came second and Private Twigg (Pianist) was third. Shortly afterwards the Royal Army Service Corps presented a revue called "This'll Shake You", with a big variety programme.

The "Thursday at Seven" concerts in the "Grand Pavilion" deserve special mention. These were first inaugurated by the Town Council in conjunction with officers of the units stationed in Porthcawl in September 1939. They continued weekly without interruption throughout the war, compered and stage-managed by Mr. Oswald Thomas, who lived in South Place. The concerts were popular with the residents and with the thousands of serving men and women who were stationed at one time or another in Porthcawl and when on 31 January 1946 the 333rd and last "Thursday at Seven" Concert with the Troops was held, it was estimated that over the previous six years 350,000 servicemen and civilians had been entertained at the concerts.

Victory in Europe on 8 May 1945 was celebrated with an impressive parade. The contingents marched from Griffin Park to St John's Church, Newton, where a Thanksgiving Service was held. The parade was lead by an R.A.F. Band which was followed by members and officials of the Urban District Council, senior officers from each of the services and contingents of the Glamorgan Constabulary, Sea Cadets, West Yorkshire Regiment, Royal Artillery, R.A.F., R.A.M.C., Free French Air Force, W.A.A.F., Home Guard, A.T.C., Observer Corps, Red Cross, Civil Defence, WVS, British Legion, Girl Guides and Boys Brigade.

In the evening, after the King's speech on the wireless to the nation, a hugh bonfire was lit on Newton Green and there was an impressive firework display, the pyrotechnics being significantly enhanced by the contribution of two young men who, it has been suggested, had raided the flare store on the Newton Rifle Range.

A special VE Dance was held in the Grand Pavilion, which was packed with dancers and spectators.

One of Porthcawl's best remembered celebrities was awarded the M.B.E. in July 1945. Captain George Stanley Pine, a garage owner of Newton, was a pioneer of flying at Porthcawl, being the founder of Pine's Airways Ltd. This operated at first from a grassed field which ran parallel with Locks Lane. Later, the airfield moved closer to the Rest Home. Pine's Airways initially consisted of one Fox-Moth aeroplane, the fleet later being expanded to two. Up and down flights from the airfield cost 2/6d (12 1/2p); over Kenfig Pool, 5/-; £1 to Nash lighthouse and £2 to fly over Cardiff or Mumbles. There is an interesting collection of Pine's Airways memorabilia, donated by Mrs Pine, in the Porthcawl Museum.

George Pine was born in Newton and attended the local Church school and later went to Newton Primary. When he left school he helped his father who ran a taxi service with a horse-drawn hansom cab and two covered cabs. Later Mr Pine's father bought a Buick car and started the Porthcawl Omnibus Company with a converted Renault called "The Toastrack" because much of the bodywork had been removed. George Pine trained at Marconi's and he made his own wireless sets which he sold in the village. He joined the British Oxygen Company for a period to learn the art of welding. In about 1932 he went to Cardiff Airport to learn flying, obtained his pilot's "A" license and then in around 1934 went to De Havilland's in Hatfield to train for his pilot's "B" License. He bought his first aircraft, a Fox Moth, for £1200. At first it was necessary for him to fly the plane every morning to Cardiff for a serviceability inspection, so Mr Pine qualified as an engineer in order that he could carry out the serviceability checks at Porthcawl.

So successful was Pine's Airways that he purchased a second Fox Moth. Alan Cobham (of "Cobham's Flying Circus"), Amy Johnson and her husband, Jim Mollinson visited the airfield. In the last week of August, 1939, 3500 passengers were carried.

At the outbreak of war the airfield was closed and the aircraft were "requisitioned". George Pine was one of the founder members of the Air Transport Auxiliary (known as the A.T.A and nicknamed the "Aged and Tired Airmen"), ferrying aircraft from factories to service airfields. When he was awarded the M.B.E. in 1945, Mr Pine was second in command of that organisation and was

George Pine with his Fox Moth at Locks Common Airfield   *Porthcawl Museum*

based at Whitchurch Airport, Bristol. He received his medal from King George VI in Cardiff Castle.

After the war ended George Pine was unable to obtain the use of the former airfield for flying and he was offered work as a test pilot at an aircraft company near Birmingham. He decided that he was too old for test flying and accepted a job in Blackpool.

At the beginning of July 1945 Porthcawl was packed with visitors. "On the beach, along the promenade, outside every cafe and milling around the station and bus stops, with luncheon baskets, thermos flasks, buckets and spades. They were brought by special trains from the Valleys and at 5 o'clock they had already started to queue for home".
Three weeks later "the biggest crowd of daytrippers Porthcawl has ever seen and who it is believed have beaten pre-war records, packed the promenades and beaches".

Members of the Free French Airforce, who were based at R.A.F. Stormy Down, celebrated Bastille Day on 14 July 1945 by holding an impressive procession through Porthcawl. R.A.F. officers and men marched with the Free French and the parade was lead by bands of the R.A.F. and W.A.A.F.. Later, sports were held at a local camp where refreshments were provided" and a good time was had by all".

In August, 1945 the Japanese surrendered and the War was over. On VJ night "the Promenade was the scene of wild excitement. People cheered and sang until their feet ached and their voices grew hoarse. Mr Deg Smith of the AFS brought a loudspeaker on to the scene to provide dance music. Street parties were held in spite of the indifference of the weather".
In September Porthcawl Urban District Council entertained over 1000 children to tea at the Grand Pavilion, followed by a concert, which included acrobats, comedians and ventriloquists supplied by the West Yorkshire Regiment's 5th Battalion.

The War might be over but the long uphill battle had begun to restore peacetime conditions. Rationing of food was to continue for many years and wartime industries had to be converted to meet the country's needs. This affected many of Porthcawl's residents who had worked at the Royal Ordnance Factory in

Bridgend making ammunition, which was now no longer needed.

A "Thanksgiving Week" was launched in October 1945 with a target of £75,000. In his speech inaugurating the Week, Lt. Col. H. St George Theyte said "During the War the people of Britain had one target - to defeat the enemy and that had been done. Not alone by the magnificent efforts of the Armed Forces but by the loyalty of the people at home. During the War no-one had to put up with more privations than the people had done. Now they have another target - to help obtain those peacetime conditions to which they are entitled".

A flight of pigeons was released from the balcony and an indicator board, which took the form of the Angel of Peace holding up the total collected, showed the first £1000 donated by the Great Western Railway. At the end of the Week the total had risen to £77,536, equivalent today to £1,460,885!

The War had brought the people of Porthcawl together in a way that has not been seen since. The anxiety of everyone to do everything they could to preserve the independence of Britain against the evils of Nazism encouraged them to join the many civilian organisations that flourished in the town. They suffered the austerities of food, fuel and clothing rationing but they were fortunately spared the blitz, the flying bombs and the V2 rockets. But the names of 41 young men on the town's war memorial show that the war had brought personal tragedy to many Porthcawl families.

The presence in the town of so many young servicemen from Britain, Holland, France, Poland, Canada and the United States acted as a powerful antidote to wartime depression. The town's character would change enormously during the next forty years and there are those who lived through the war years in Porthcawl who remember them with warm nostalgia, recapturing, perhaps, the golden days of their youth but possibly also recalling that fleeting moment when the town was for once, more or less, wholly united.

CHAPTER TWO

THE HOME GUARD

In May 1940, with the threat of an invasion by German forces seeming to be an imminent probability, a decision was taken by the War Cabinet to strengthen the Regular and Territorial Army by recruiting civilian men between the ages of 17 and 65, who were not already engaged in civil defence activities. The new force was called the Local Defence Volunteers and by July 1940 it had grown nationally to number some one and half million men; in that month it was renamed the "Home Guard".

In Porthcawl many men who were in reserved occupations or who were too young, too old or who were otherwise unable to join one of the Regular armed services, reported in May 1940 to the Police Station in John Street for enrolment in the Local Defence Volunteers. Mr Ben H Clarke, who now lives in Ely, Cambridgeshire, had come to Wales in 1937 as a surveyor working with Sir Linday Parkinson on the construction of the Royal Arsenal at Bridgend. In 1940 he was lodging in the "Stoneleigh", which was at that time a private house owned by Mr & Mrs Telford Davies.

"I heard the appeal on the wireless from the War Minister, Anthony Eden, and I immediately went to the Police Station in John Street to enrol", recalls Mr Clarke. "The first LDV units were very democratic, electing their own leaders. We reported once a week at the Seabank Hotel, where we received elementary training and were drilled by a Senior NCO from the South Wales Borderers. Our duties were mainly to man an observation post on the coast between Porthcawl and Ogmore on a nightly roster system after having reported to the Police Station and been issued with a 12 bore shotgun. There was only a handful of guns at the Police Station and the majority of the volunteers armed themselves with pick helves. We had no uniforms".

Mr Clarke remembers reporting with others to Ewenny Bridge when the air raid alarm sounded and on one occasion stopping a coach and demanding to see the identity cards of the occupants. "The driver asked to see my written authority to inspect the passengers' identity cards. This could not be produced as no such documents had been issued and we hastily withdrew"!

"Dad's Army" - Porthcawl's Home Guard.
No.1 Platoon, "A" Company, 24th Glamorgan (Kenfig) Battalion on parade outside their Headquarters in Picton Avenue, Porthcawl.
Porthcawl Museum

"We were a conscientious and devoted bunch of volunteers who enjoyed our duties," recalls Mr Clarke. "Very often met after duty for drinks in the "Rock" public house". Mr Clarke left Porthcawl for service in the Army just before the LDV became the Home Guard in July 1940.

Mr Morgan Joseph, who lives at Ty Coch, Porthcawl, also joined the Local Defence Volunteers in May 1940 and remained a member of the Home Guard throughout the war. The Home Guard unit in Porthcawl was No 1 Platoon, "A" Company of the 24th Glamorgan (Kenfig) Battalion, whose first Headquarters were in the garages that used to be at the rear of the Seabank Hotel. Later the Headquarters were transferred to the Pier Hotel and to a cafe on Coney Beach before moving to a house in Picton Avenue; a photograph survives of the platoon assembled in front of the house. The Commanding Officer of the Bridgend area was Colonel H.M. Llewellyn of Court Coleman and the Officers and N.C.O.s of the Porthcawl platoon were all ex-servicemen from the First World War. The local Commander was Colonel Evans, other officers being Major F C Ashton, Captain Duncan Thomas, Captain Cartwright, who later transferred to the Mounted Home Guard and was replaced by Lieutenant D M Evans Bevan. Captain Firstbrook was an attached Officer and the Sergeant Major was Joe Saunders, assisted by Sergeant Bass and Sergeant Bill Oliver, who was later commissioned as a Lieutenant. The Quartermasters were Lee McKewan, F Rogers and D Jenkins.

Initially, as also recalled by Mr Clarke, the Platoon was only equipped with shot-guns and staves, although the Nottage section, under Captain Duncan Thomas, had two rifles and nearly everyone had a shotgun. In the early days arm-bands were worn but these were replaced with denims and later by full battle-dress uniforms and great-coats. In November, 1940, it was announced by the War Office that 500,000 showerproof capes made of battle-dress material would be issued to the Home Guard throughout the U.K. in addition to the 650,000 great coats already issued. The shortage of rifles remained a problem until shipments of arms arrived from the United States and Canada and these, together with their ammunition, were kept in safe places when not required for guard duty and parades. The Nottage section, for example, kept their rifles in Nottage Court.

After their Headquarters at the Seabank had been taken over by the Regular Army, the Porthcawl platoon paraded in front of the Rest Home. A disused furniture repository in West End Avenue, Nottage, was also used by the Home Guard until it, also, was occupied by the Army.

The first assignment of the newly formed Local Defence Force unit was to man an observation post at Candleston Farm, Tythegston, and the railway bridge at North Cornelly which carried the main line to Paddington. Later, the platoon guarded the Home Guard Headquarters in Picton Avenue and the telephone exchange which at that time was housed in 24, Victoria Avenue. When the Llynfi Power Station was built, the Porthcawl platoon took its turn in a rota, providing guard cover for this vulnerable service and also for the Coytrahen Explosives Experimental area.

As .22 Rifle Range at Dan-y-graig was used by the LDV until the Dutch Army arrived at the Dan-y-graig Camp in June 1940 and took it over. The Dutch were a welcome source of supply for Luger pistols; members of the Home Guard bought the pistols and ammunition for £1. The .303 range on Newton Burrows was also used by the Porthcawl platoon and many of the men were excellent shots. There were regular competitions against the R.A.F. Regiment from Stormy Down, the Post Office Platoon and a platoon from Bridgend, which the Porthcawl platoon regularly won. The Nottage Section had monthly .22 competitions with the Porthcawl Police and the Home Guard always won. "It was a pleasure to take the shilling a head wager from the police", recalled Mr Morgan Joseph, who was a Sergeant in the Home Guard in 1942 and was promoted to 2nd Lieutenant in April 1944.

There was keen rivalry between the Platoons and the Nottage Section was particularly successful. On one occasion, in 1944, it had the task of "capturing" Llantrisant Railway Station, which was being guarded by the Cowbridge Platoon. The Nottage Section waded down the Ely River and took the Station's defenders completely by surprise.

In 1943, the Porthcawl Platoon won the "Colonel Main" Cup in the South Wales District Competition and the "Colonel Otto Jones" Cup in the Glamorgan Competition in Battle Platoon Firing, held at Brecon. It was described in the "South Wales News" of September 15 as "One of the biggest military competitions ever staged" and included tests of field craft, initiative, leadership and marksmanship. Practically every Home Guard Company, from Monmouthshire

Porthcawl Museum

Winners of the "Colonel Main Cup", Porthcawl Home Guard - 1943

J. Barry Jones

Porthcawl's Home Guard Mounted Patrol.

to West Wales took part and the eliminating progress took all summer. More than 1000 platoons went through a stiff battle course, "evidence of the practical training of the Home Guard these days".

Certificates were presented afterwards in the Grand Pavilion to those who had taken part by the Commanding Officer of the British Home Forces, who remarked that the men were as fit as any platoon in the British Army.

The photograph of the Porthcawl Platoon taken in the Coney Beach fun fair in 1943 shows that the unit was reasonably well armed with Lewis guns, Bren guns and Sten guns. Sergeant G. Morgan Joseph can be seen on the extreme right of the second row.

Although, thanks to the BBC programme "Dad's Army", most people have an awareness of the Home Guard (although it gives a somewhat unfairly comical view of what was unquestionably a highly trained effective force), very few are aware that the Home Guard also maintained a mounted force.

The Porthcawl Mounted Section was formed in 1942, and was an off-shoot of the Cowbridge platoon which had been organised under Colonel Homfrey, Master of the Glamorgan Hunt, who had served in the Yeomanry in the First World War. Another member of the Cowbridge Mounted Home Guard was Mr Edwin Hardy, who had also served in the Yeomanry and who had a butcher's shop in what is now the Sub-Post Office in Newton, and it was he who formed the Porthcawl Mounted Section. Unfortunately Mr Hardy died suddenly and the platoon was taken over by Mr Reg Elcock, who held the rank of Captain. Mr Elcock built the original garage opposite to the Globe Inn. After a short period the platoon was taken over by Mr Mark Dawe, who lived at "Tournai" West Road, Nottage and he built the strength of the unit up to about 30.

Initially, the unit met every Sunday morning in riding stables close to Crown House, Newton, but when Sergeant Dawe took charge, the platoon assembled in a field at the back of "Tournai", Nottage. Mr Dawe had his own stables there, with twelve horses. In addition, the section carried out foot training with the Porthcawl platoon.

The main activity of the mounted section was to patrol Merthyr Mawr Warren and to provide safety patrols around Rest Bay when the Army was firing out to sea. The section also rode out over Margam and Sker. A photograph taken in 1942 shows eight of the platoon mounted in the field adjacent to "Tournai", with Sergeant Mark Dawe on the extreme left, accompanied by Ray Rees, Charles E Jones, "Spadge" John, Arthur Jones, "Arty" Hanbury, Ivor Thomas and J Barry Jones, who provided the information for this account of the mounted patrol.

On 6 December, 1944, H.M. King George VI, who was Colonel - in - Chief of the Home Guard, issued the following message:-

"For more than four years you have borne a heavy burden. Most of you have been engaged for long hours in work necessary to the prosecution of the war or to maintaining the healthful life of the Nation; and you have given every portion of your time which should have been your own to learning the skilled worked of a soldier. By this patient, ungrudging effort you have built and maintained a force able to play an essential part in the defence of our threatened soil and liberty.

I have long wished to see you relieved of this burden; but it would have been a betrayal of all we owe to our fathers and our sons if any step had been taken which might have imperilled our Country's safety. A slackening of our defenses might have encouraged the enemy to launch a desperate blow which could grievously have damaged us and weakened the power of our own assault. Now, at last, the splendid resolution and endurance of the Allied Armies have thrust back that danger from our coasts. At last I can say that you have fulfilled your charge.

The Home Guard has reached the end of its long tour of duty under arms. But I know that your devotion to our land, your comradeship, your power to work your hardest at the end of the longest day, will discover new outlets for patriotic service in the time of peace. History will say that your share in the greatest of all our struggles for freedom was a vitally important one. You have earned in full measure your country's gratitude".

CHAPTER THREE

THE ROYAL OBSERVER CORPS

Hidden away in the field next to Locks Lane was, until April 1994, an underground operations room which had acquired a certain mystique amongst the residents of Porthcawl, some of whom believed it to be the entrance to an immense underground bunker to be used by the favoured few following an atomic attack. The bunker, in fact, was built in 1961 on the site of a wartime surface observation post, and consisted of an entrance turret, topped by a locked hinged plate which when lifted revealed a ladder. The underground chamber, covered by 3 feet of reinforced concrete, was 12 feet below ground. At the foot of the ladder was a small recessed area that housed an Elsan toilet and to the right was a door leading to a small room, measuring approximately 8 ft x 12 ft. The post was occupied from 1961 until it was disbanded on 30 September 1991 by men of the Royal Observer Corps, who operated a continuous 8 hour shift pattern, each with two men, whose duty it was to check for radioactive fall-out in the event of a nuclear attack.

The original observation post was a wooden structure, built in 1938 for what was then the Observer Corps. The basis of the Corps, (whose badge depicts an Elizabethan beacon lighter which alludes to the warning system of invasion used in the sixteenth century) can be traced to 1914, when the police were instructed to telephone reports of any Zeppelins or aircraft seen or heard within 60 miles of London to the Admiralty, who at that time were responsible for Britain's defenses. The War Office took over this responsibility in 1917 but the system of co-ordinated coastal and inland posts, searchlights, gun stations, balloon aprons etc did not come into operation until September 1918 and as the last German raids had taken place in the previous May, there was no opportunity to test its effectiveness. At the end of the First World War the system faded away but in 1924 it was agreed that an organised system for the rapid collection and distribution of information on the movements of both friendly and hostile aircraft was essential. The area between Romney Marshes and Tonbridge in Kent was chosen for the first experiments and three other areas in the south of England were later brought into the scheme.

The Air Ministry took over control in 1929 and the Observer Corps became a cor-

Home Office

The R.O.C. Post after the war.

porate body, with a Commandant of Air Commodore rank appointed from the retired list. There was no expansion in the organisation, however, until the political situation in Europe worsened and from 1935 new groups were formed. By the time the Corps was mobilised on 24 August 1939 the greater part of the country was covered by Observer Corps posts which identified the type, numbers, height and flight path of enemy aircraft crossing the coast and formed an essential part of the defence system. The reports were integrated with the information obtained from Radar stations and enable R.A.F controllers in Operations Rooms to be fully aware of the extent of enemy incursions and made possible a greater number of interceptions.

Air raid warning officers were also installed in Observer Corps centres to give warning of imminent attack to vital industrial undertakings, saving millions of man hours of productive factory time which would otherwise have been lost had workers taken to the shelters each time a general air raid alarm been sounded.

On 9 April 1941 it was announced that His Majesty King George VI had granted permission for the Corps to use the title "Royal" and in September 1941 women were introduced into the Corps. In 1942 there were extensive changes to the organisation, the first being to adjust each area to conform to the Fighter Group with which it was concerned. This did not affect Porthcawl which was under Group 25, under the call sign "G-George 3" from the time it became operational in 1938 until it transferred to 13 Group in 1953, when 25 Group was disbanded. Headquarters of 25 Group was in Cardiff; from 1938 - 1940 it was at the Westgate Street GPO and it then moved to Insole Court, Llandaff until 1943 when it was transferred to Ely Rise, Llandaff. It remained there until 1946 when it moved to RAF Caerau, Ely, Cardiff. The Group was disbanded in the reorganisation of 1953 and Porthcawl was transferred in November to 13 Group, with its Headquarters in Carmarthen, under the call sign J-Juliet 3. When the underground post became operational in 1961, when its function was the measurement of radio-active fall-out rather than the tracking of enemy aircraft, it remained in 13 Group but its call sign was changed in October 1968 to L-Lima 3 and was again changed the following year to L-Lima 2. The underground post remained in use until the Corps was disbanded in 1991. It was finally demolished in April 1994.

The observation post at Porthcawl, which was commissioned in 1938, consisted

Royal Observer Corps post at Locks Lane, Porthcawl.

Porthcawl Museum

Chief Observer, Walter Lang, in the observation tower.

Porthcawl Museum

of a wooden shed, topped by a tower giving an excellent view over the Bristol Channel. It was continuously manned, day and night, initially under the command of an Observer Group Officer, reporting to a centre controller in Cardiff. In 1942 this changed when a Group Commandant was appointed to unify the policy within each Group. A Deputy was also appointed and an adjutant was made responsible for Group administration. Observer Officers were appointed to take charge of the posts. The training was standardised throughout the Corps and at each post an observer was appointed as a training instructor with the rank of Leading Observer. The head Observer at each post was given the rank of "Chief Observer" and he was responsible to his Group Officer for the administration of his post.

Sadly, it has not been possible to talk to any of the Observers who manned the wooden observation post during the war years; it appears that there are no survivors from those times.

The Royal Observer Corps made a further significant contribution to victory by its participation in "Operation Overlord", the invasion by the Allies of Nazi occupied Europe in June 1944. The C in C of the Allied Air Force, Air Chief Marshal Sir Trafford Leigh-Mallory, expressed concern at the number of friendly aircraft that were being shot down. The solution adopted was for observers trained in aircraft recognition to sail with and to advise gun crews on board ships taking part in the invasion. The observers required to man the ships were drawn from some 1400 members of the Corps who volunteered for this duty. Ten of them were mentioned in despatches and subsequently King George VI approved the wearing of the shoulder badge "Seaborne". An interesting footnote to this is that Mr Ken Baker, who was a member of the 49th West Riding Reconnaissance Regiment which was formed in Porthcawl and spent twelve months in the town, recalled that as he was crossing the Channel shortly after D-Day he was chatting to one of these Seaborne Observers and asked him where he came from. "Oh, you won't have heard of my home town", said the Observer "I come from a little town on the south coast of Wales - Porthcawl!" There were several Observers from Porthcawl who were entitled to proudly wear the Seaborne badge.

CHAPTER FOUR

THE BRITISH ARMY

15th Battalion The Welch Regiment

In March 1939, as the war clouds darkened over Europe, the Government decided to double the strength of the Territorial Army. It designated the newly formed battalions by the prefix 2/ in front of the existing battalion number and so the 2/4 (i.e. the second fourth) battalion of the Welch Regiment was formed. It joined the 2/5 Battalion and the 4th Battalion of the Monmouthshire Regiment to form the 113th Infantry Brigade of the 38th (Welsh) Division.

Not long after its formation the 2/4th was re-numbered the 15th Battalion, the Welsh Regiment. This was because of pressure to preserve a connection with the Carmarthenshire Battalion of World War `1 and the people of Carmarthen responded to the restoration of the link with the County by donating a complete set of band instruments to the new Battalion. Many of the new recruits came from the Carmarthen area although in some cases they just happened to be living in the town at the time. The Rev. Vernon Jones, who now lives in Porthcawl, was a student at the Carmarthen Teacher Training College in 1938, at the start of a three year course. He recalled that ninety students joined the Territorials on the promise that if they did so they would be allowed to complete their teacher training course before being called up. He and his fellow students attended the summer training camp at Dan-y-graig, Porthcawl in August, 1939, and returned home but on 29 August, two days later, there was general mobilisation and, all promises of deferment forgotten, the students found themselves back in Dan-y-graig camp with the 15th Battalion, the Welch Regiment.

The newly formed Battalion suffered from a serious shortage of efficient instructors, equipment and clothing and because of the lack of military vehicles a number of civilian vans and lorries were commandeered. In spite of these difficulties, there was great enthusiasm. Initially the men were dispersed to vulnerable points throughout South Wales but as these responsibilities were taken over by other units, they returned to Dan-y-graig to continue their training.

The 15th Battalion remained in Porthcawl throughout the winter of 1939-40; they were housed initially in tents but later they billeted in the bowling alley of the General Picton pub and in the Coney Beach fun fair.

Early in June 1940, 2000 men of the British Expeditionary Force arrived in Porthcawl from the beaches of Dunkirk and the 15th Battalion was assigned the responsibility of organising their reception and accommodation. The survivors from Dunkirk were dirty and exhausted. Many of Porthcawl's residents remember seeing them stretched out on the Esplanade. Others took them into their homes, whilst some were accommodated in an old furniture warehouse in Nottage Village.

Not long after the Dunkirk survivors had left Porthcawl, 1460 men of the Royal Dutch Army arrived and the 15th Battalion was involved in the logistics of arranging accommodation and food for them. It was also assigned the responsibility for the defence of the R.A.F. airfields at St. Athan and Llandow and because of this the Battalion Headquarters moved from Danygraig to Llantwit Major.

This was the end of the Battalion's association with Porthcawl. In August, 1940, it moved with the 38th Division to a tented camp near Rugely in Staffordshire and in November of that year it transferred to Ramillies Barracks in Aldershot for intensive training. The Battalion was given a counter-attack role and was allocated a defensive area on the South Downs to deal with any invasion landing.

The 38th Division's establishment was reduced to providing beach defence and to the training of recruits for other formations and from November 1941 to May 1943 it was stationed in Dorset. In May, 1943, the 15th Battalion was involved in the organisation and conduct of "Operation Harlequin", the full scale rehearsal of the invasion of Europe. In October 1943 the Battalion moved to Hertford and shortly afterwards to Northumberland, where it acted as the "enemy" for troops of the Second British Army. In January 1944 the Battalion transferred to Scapa Flow in the Orkney Isles, where it formed the defence garrison. Finally, the Battalion was despatched to Ballyedmon in Northern Ireland, where it was used as a training and draft finding unit until it finally disbanded.

Few, if any, of the soldiers who joined the 15th Battalion in 1939 remained with it throughout the war. Most and probably all were posted to other Battalions of the Welch Regiment and many were transferred to other arms and units of the British

Army. The role of the 15th was that of a defensive and recruit training arm of the Army, an essential function but one that denied it the opportunity of battle honours.

49th West Riding Reconnaisance Regiment

A tablet on the wall inside St John's Church, Newton, records the 50th Anniversary of the formation in September 1942 in Porthcawl of the 49th West Riding Reconnaisance Regiment. The tablet was dedicated on 6 September 1992, and the service was attended by many former members of the Regiment and by many residents, including the Town's Mayor, Mrs Madeline Moon.

The 49th (West Riding) Division was a pre-war Territorial Army formation, which consisted of three Brigades, the 146th, 147th and 148th. The first two recruited in Yorkshire and the 148th in the Nottingham and Derby area. In 1940 the 49th Division was involved in the disastrous campaign in Norway and the 148th Brigade suffered severe casualties and was replaced by 70 Brigade, another Territorial Army unit which recruited in the Tyneside area. The Division was then ordered to occupy Iceland and it took as its Divisional sign the Polar Bear.

In 1942 the 49th Division returned to England and was earmarked for the Normandy invasion which was to take place in 1944. Whilst in Iceland it had no requirement for a Reconnaissance Regiment, but in view of its new role it became an essential provision.

Meanwhile the Reconnaissance Corps had been formed in 1941 to carry out the duties of reconnaissance in front of the Infantry. This was the role that had been undertaken by the Light Cavalry in the 18th and 19th Centuries. The Reconnaissance Corps was composed of various Regiments and Independent Squadrons and in the summer of 1942 it was to amalgamate three of the latter to form the Regiment that was required by the 49th Division. In accordance with the normal practice in such cases the Reconnaissance Regiment was given the same number as the Division in which it was to serve - the 49th.

The 29th and 148th Independent Squadrons arrived in Porthcawl in September 1942 and they became "A" and "B" Squadrons. The 1st Belgian Fusiliers originally formed "C" Squadron but in December 1942 they were replaced by the 24th

(Guards) Independent Squadron.

It can therefore be seen that the 49th West Riding Reconnaissance did not come from any particular area and had little or no connection with Yorkshire. The men were specially selected for various skills, irrespective of their places of birth. Some were required to know all about wireless, the mainstay of reconnaissance. Others would be required to be able to drive any type of vehicle. They would need to be capable of finding their way about strange countryside and there would be men trained to clear minefields and to hit both men and aircraft from the revolving turret of an armoured car.

Possibly the hardest task of all was that of the Reconnaissance Regiment's assault troopers. When the main attack force was held up in battle, it was the job of the assault troopers to move up in speedy little trucks and clear away the opposition. These men were required to be capable of making their way at top speed over any kind of country and to fight as they went. They had to be able to dig the first stages of a trench system in half the normal time. Their weapon training was to an extremely high level; troopers were sent round a "blitz" range to be "attacked" at various points, sometimes so suddenly that they had to fire their service rifles from the hip.

The 49th Reconnaissance Regiment spent its time in Porthcawl undergoing intensive training. Individual fitness was a high priority, with physical training on the sands and cross country runs over the sand dunes which then extended beyond Coney Beach. The Regiment imposed a high standard of turn-out and drill and the evening guard mounting parades in front of the Esplanade Hotel drew large crowds of onlookers. There were gun drill exercises by the Regiment's Anti-Tank Battery on the Common opposite the Seabank Hotel and the unit took part in a number of training exercises in the Black Mountains and the Brecon Beacons, with the Anti-Tank guns travelling to Harlech to practice on dummy tanks.

The Regiment remained in Porthcawl until the summer of 1943. During that time it established a warm relationship with the townspeople and eleven members of the unit married Porthcawl girls. When the Regiment moved out of the town it went first to Scotland and then to Norfolk and joined the invasion of Normandy shortly after D-Day.

The 49th Reconnaissance Regiment was involved in fighting from the time it landed. At first it was employed in a purely infantry role, protecting the Divisional left flank. The Anti-Tank gun training on The Green in Porthcawl was soon rewarded when the troop of anti-tank guns under "B" Squadron command knocked out four German tanks in one engagement on the outskirts of Fontenay. It took until August 15th before the Regiment could assume its real job of reconnoitring in front of the Division. During the following fortnight the Regiment would advance ahead of the Infantry, take prisoners, examine the condition of bridges and report on the positions held by the enemy. On August 25th the Germans made a determined stand near Epaignes but they were finally beaten back by the combined efforts of the three Squadrons. "A" Squadron crossed the Seine at the end of August on rafts, but two bren-gun carriers were lost in the river when the rafts capsized. The remainder of the Regiment abandoned the crossing and headed for the bridge at Bolbec, which was found to be leaning drunkenly into the river at a very steep angle and littered with masses of German equipment, motor transport and dead horses. In spite of these obstructions, the Regiment crossed over and headed for Le Havre, brushing aside some of the outer defenses and capturing an entire company of Germans, before handing over the task of dealing with the stronger resistance to the Division.

The Regiment was heavily involved in the battles that were fought throughout the remainder of the war; on 14 April 1945 it passed through Arnhem and as the war ended on 8 May 1945 it made a sweep through the countryside that became a triumphal march. The greetings of the wildly enthusiastic Dutch people was something that those who were with the Regiment at that time would never forget.

5th Battalion The West Yorkshire Regiment

It has proved impossible to obtain an "official" history of this unit, although there are several references to the part it played in the community life of Porthcawl. Mr W E "Chalky" White, who now lives in Oxenhope, West Yorkshire, arrived here in 1944 and says that it was the 2/5th Battalion that was formed in Porthcawl, the 1/5th having been wiped out in the Far East. He was amongst the first of the new Battalion to arrive in the town and he was initially billeted in the Seabank and later moved to the Esplanade, where the HQ Company was set up. Mr White was in the Signals Company and was reserve drummer in the "West Yorks Dance Band", which played mainly in the "Cosy Corner Cafe". The Band is also mentioned in a "Glamorgan Gazette" report of a successful dance in the Pavilion on 18 July 1945, when "600 people danced to the music of Mrs Morgan's Band, augmented for the occasion by instrumentalists of the 5th Battalion, West Yorkshire Regiment". However, these musicians did not include Mr White, who by then was serving in Italy and later, in Austria with the main body of the Battalion.

The Battalion spent its time here undergoing training in beach landings on Coney Beach and "desert" fighting around Kenfig. On one occasion, in the early hours of the morning, Mr White was buried up to his neck when a trench collapsed and he thought his end had come. The Battalion also practiced landing and assault from the lake at Kenfig. "The idea was to make us into a light mobile Battalion, able to pack up and move in a very few hours".

Mr White remembers a stabbing that took place in the "Grand Pavilion" one Saturday night. "A local lad was stabbed by a "Free French" airman about a local girl. All hell had let loose; the two local policemen available could not calm the situation. Soldiers of the 5th Battalion who were on duty in the Esplanade Hotel, were asked to help the police out. Armed with pick axe shafts we surrounded the Pavilion, went in and rounded up all the Free French airmen and marched them out of Porthcawl on to the road to Stormy Down, where they were billeted. The town was placed out of bounds to them for a while". This incident was also recalled by Mr Ken Carr, who now lives in Leeds and who was stationed in Porthcawl at the same time. He was billeted in "the wooden huts up the road from the Pavilion, but other soldiers were accommodated in houses and hotels", and remembers the closed pubs on Sundays and special weekend passes to the Rhondda Valley where there was a warm welcome in the Miners' Clubs.

In late October, 1944, the 2/5th Battalion left overnight from Porthcawl Station and travelled to Glasgow Docks, embarking on a troopship, equipped in tropical clothing. Two days later the men were told that their destination was Italy and the tropical gear was exchanged for battledress. The troopship landed in Naples and the various companies were dispersed. Mr White's company guarded a big food dump which held stores for all the Central Mediteranean forces. "We had regular battles with the black market Mafia", he recalls. In January, 1946 the Battalion moved to Austria, where they assumed the duties of border guards. The remnants of the 1st Battalion were later merged with the 5th, and subsequently the West Yorkshire Regiment became part of the Prince of Wales's Own Regiment of Yorkshire.

4th Monmouthshire Battalion.

The 4th Monmouthshire Battalion was created during the doubling of the Territorial Army in 1939. On 13 August, 1939, the Battalion was in camp at Dan-y-graig, Porthcawl, with 17 officers and about 550 other ranks. Equipment was very scarce; what there was had been borrowed from the 2nd Battalion which had been in camp prior to the 4th's arrival, and consisted of a bren-gun carrier, a 15cwt truck, one 3" mortar, six bren guns and some requisitioned civilian vehicles. On 27th August the men dispersed back to their homes but at 8 p.m. that night a "pyjama" conference was held in Pontypool and within 24 hours the whole Battalion was mustered, with the help of the police who visited hundreds of homes. In the early hours of 29th August the 4th Monmouthshires returned to Dan-y-graig Camp, Porthcawl, where it was assigned vulnerable points to guard. "A" and "B" Companies went to the Royal Ordnance Factory at Hereford, "C" Company to the Monmouthshire end of the Severn Tunnel and "D" and part of "HQ" Companies were allocated Cardiff Docks. The most serious problem encountered was that throughout these scattered detachments not a single cook could be found and reliance had to be placed on unskilled volunteers.

By the middle of October the Battalion Headquarters had moved to the Miners' Rest Home, Rest Bay, and had also taken over other billets including Ocean View. During the winter, because of the demands of guarding the vulnerable areas, only new recruits received any training. Responsibility for the Severn Tunnel and R.O.F Hereford was taken over by other units in November but in their places the Battalion were assigned the oil works at Llandovery and the Ordnance factory at Bridgend. It also sent its first draft of two officers and 90 other ranks to the 1st South Wales Borderers in India.

In January and March 1940 men with Territorial Army training joined the battalion and later these were joined by 100 recruits from London, bringing the unit up to strength. Responsibility for guarding the vulnerable points was also taken over by other units and this enabled training to begin in earnest.

Mr T.A. Davies, of Houghton le Spring, Tyne & Wear, joined the 4th Monmouths in October 1939 and remembers being met at Porthcawl Station late at night by an RSM with lamps and marched to the Rest. He was put with an old regular sergeant in the ration stores, drawing supplies from the RASC and NAAFI and distributing them to the units. "One day, chap comes off the golf course behind the Rest and mentioned that barrels of Guiness had been washed up on the beach. Llew Morgan, the butcher and I went down and managed to get a barrel to the stores. Llew was an old soldier, so he put it in the ration stores, not the butcher's stores. I think it held 36 gallons. The previous miners' canteen had left empty bottles so I started bottling and drinking the Guiness with other pals and being green to Army Regulations, I got into trouble and was sent back to the Company platoon, which was much harder than being in the Ration store".

The story of the beached barrels of Guiness is Porthcawl's equivalent of "Whisky Galore!" On 3 March, 1940 the S.S. 'Cato II', a 710 ton cargo steamship that had been built in Cambeltown in 1914, struck a magnetic mine a few miles off Nash Point and sank. Thirteen of her crew of fifteen were drowned. The ship was carrying its regular consignment of barrels of concentrated Guiness from Dublin and many of these were washed up along the coastline. Customs moved in quickly to break up the barrels, but they did not find all of them and many found their way into the hands of appreciative imbibers. One of these was a Pyle resident who succeeded in rolling a barrel all the way from the beach to his house, where he emptied the contents into his bath. Sadly his wife was so infuriated with the sight of the brown liquid that she pulled the plug and he lost the lot!

Mr Colin Walker, who was an R.A.F. electrician at Stormy Down, told me that the R.A.F. found a barrel on the beach at Margam. An aircraft made a "forced" landing nearby and a tent was erected, ostensibly to service the defective engine, but in reality to hide the barrel until it could be transported by lorry to the aerodrome, where the contents were shared amongst three messes. He also recalled that the Air Sea Rescue boats collected 15 or so barrels from the sea and that three were buried amongst the sand-hills of Newton Burrows and never recovered.

In early June the 4th Monmouthshires shared with the Welch Regiment's 15th Battalion the responsibility of dealing with the 2000 troops who had been evacuated from Dunkirk and one of these, Drill Sergeant Shimmans of the Coldstream Guards, later returned to become Regimental Sergeant Major of the Battalion. Training again suffered when the threat of imminent invasion required the Battalion to form a "flying column" and a "stand-to" company. On several occasions the flying column rushed off in buses to deal with reports of landings of enemy parachute troops. The company was confined to the area of Battalion

Headquarters and was stood to on all air-raid alerts during its tour of 24 hours duty. During the period of invasion threat all ranks had to carry arms when walking out and "the local publicans were most helpful in furnishing the Orderly Room each morning with the numbers of the rifles left on the premises the previous night"!

During two or three months of the summer of 1940, two companies of the 4th Monmouths were stationed at R.A.F Stormy Down and constructed most of defenses there. The defence posts were manned and patrols provided by the Battalion.

On August Bank Holiday, 1940, the 4th Monmouthshire Battalion moved out of Porthcawl to Ingestre Park, near Rugeley in Staffordshire. The movement was by road and the transport consisted of vehicles requisitioned from civilian firms and private owners, varying from a shabby four-seater for the Commanding Officer to light grocer's vans and furniture pantechnicons. In October the Battalion moved to Northwich, Cheshire and after three weeks it was transferred to Aldershot to join the 38th (Welsh) Division in reserve for coastal defence. Training was intensified and in July 1941 the Battalion moved to Brighton, with responsibility for guarding the coast from Brighton to Newhaven.

During the winter of 1941 the Battalion moved into Swanage, Dorset, again with coastal defence responsibilities and also with the specific duty of guarding the Radio Location Station at Kingston.

The only action experienced by the Battalion was on the night of 27/28 February, 1942, when the Anti-Aircraft Platoon took part in a raid by parachute troops on a German Radio location post at Bruneval on the French coast. Their task was to protect the embarkation of the paratroopers into the small craft which were to bring them back after the raid. The paratroopers succeeded in destroying the post, capturing vital parts of the German apparatus together with a few prisoners, but they had to fight their way back through the Germans holding the beaches. The covering fire given by the soldiers in the small craft was of significant help in getting the paratroopers off the beach.

The Battalion moved to Poole in April 1942 and whilst there gave assistance when the dock area was heavily bombed; "A" Company was particularly praised for preventing much fire damage by its quick action in dealing with incendiary bombs. In August the unit moved again, this time to Blandford. By now it was seriously weakened in strength by having to supply drafts for overseas and with only "HQ", "A" and "S" Companies at full strength. It moved to Wimbourne Minster in October 1942 and on 15 December it lost its identity as the 4th Monmouths and became the 1st Battalion The South Wales Borderers.

CHAPTER FIVE

R.A.F. STORMY DOWN

On 1 June 1939 No 9 Armament Training School opened at a new grass airfield, just off the A48 and close to Pyle, near Porthcawl. Work had begun on the construction of the RAF Station in March 1938, the main contractors being Garrard & Sons of Manchester, and it cost a total of £280,000. The only permanent brick buildings were residences for the Station Commander and the Senior Medical Officer, together with Married Quarters for two Warrant Officers and 14 Airmen. Of the latter, all had to be at least 26 years of age. The main accommodation was provided in wooden huts.

On 20 June, the Air Officer Commanding, Air Marshall Sir C S Burnett flew in to inspect the new station, which was identified as R.A.F. Newton Down, Pyle, Nr. Bridgend.

On 31 July the Advanced Training Squadron of No 5 Flying Training School Sealand was attached to the station and remained until 25 August, when it was replaced by No 3 Flying Training School, from South Cerney.

The Station was transferred to war establishment on 1 September, 1939 and the formation was announced of No 7 Air Observers School.

As war was declared on 3 September between Great Britain and Germany, a detachment of 10 Westland Wallace aircraft and 5 Hawker Henleys arrived from No 1, Air Observers School, North Coates, together with 9 Officers and 39 Other Ranks. 4 Fairy Battle aircraft joined the Station on 5 September from Little Rissington and on 11 September 60 airmen Wireless Operators arrived from R.A.F. Yatesbury for air gunners training, forming No 1 Course.

The short lived stay of No 3 FTS ended on 17 September, when the aircraft of the Advanced Training Squadron returned to South Cerney.

No 1 Air Gunners Course ended on 7 October; 58 out of the 60 on the course passed, the newly qualified Wireless Operator/Air Gunners dispersing to active squadrons. No 2 course began on 9 October with only 30 students and on 16

RAF Stormy Down in 1946
© Crown Copyright / M.O.D. Reproduced with the permission of the Controller of HMSO

Porthcawl Museum

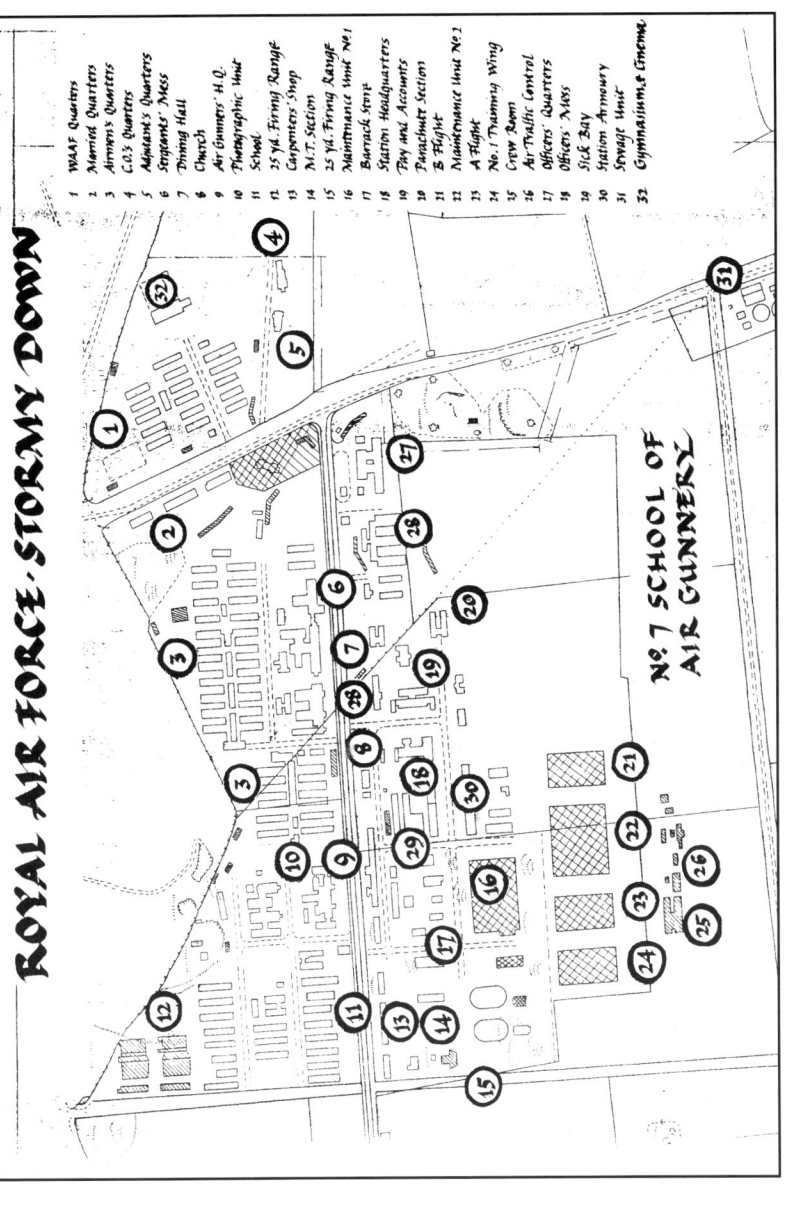

Royal Air Force, Stormy Down.

October, the first Air Observers Course began.

On 21 October, 1939, No 2 Advanced Training School arrived, with 9 twin-engined Oxford and 10 Harvard training aircraft. The 37 officer trainees were accommodated at the Seabank Hotel.

By 27 October the aircraft complement consisted of 9 Handley Page Harrows, 4 Fairy Battles, 12 Hawker Henleys, 1 Miles Magister and 10 Westland Wallaces; three of the Harrows were transferred to R.A.F. Farnborough on 6 December for anti-submarine work and were replaced by three Whitley bombers.

The Free French Air Force was later to play a significant part in the story of the airfield; the Station was visited on 14 December by Commandant Chassis who came to discuss the possibility of training French Air Observers, Air Gunners and Advanced Training Squadrons. However, it was not until November 1944 that No 23 (French) Initial Training Wing was transferred from RAF Filey to Stormy Down.

The extremely cold conditions at the aerodrome in January 1940 were vividly recalled recently by Air Chief Marshal Sir Ruthven Wade. As a young officer, he was posted to the Station at that time, flying open cockpit Westland Wallace biplanes."It was one of the coldest winters I can remember" , he said. "There was freezing rain for ten days and we were living in huts some 200 yards from the mess. When you went to the mess, after about 100 yards you began to crackle and by the time you arrived you were covered with a film of ice".

The Air Chief Marshal also remembered Wing Commander Ira ("Taffy") Jones who was Officer Commanding Flying. "Taffy" Jones was a World War 1 flying ace, and wore the DSO and bar, the MC and Bar, the DFC and the Military Medal. He suffered from a "ferocious stutter" and was, inspite of his successes in knocking enemy aircraft out of the sky, not a very good pilot. He would sit in the bar, reminiscing "I s-s-s-shot down 43 H-H-H-Huns and I was either s-s-shot down or crashed 42 times, so I reckoned that by the end of the war I was one up!"

He was greatly respected and liked by those under his command and this respect was considerably enhanced when he took off in an unarmed Hawker Henley and pursued a Ju 88 that was in the process of bombing Swansea. Jones dived on the

Hawker 'Henley'.   *RAF Museum P3006*

A 'Harrow' Bomber at Stormy Down airfield.   *Colin Walker.*

Fairey 'Battle' prepares to take off from Stormy Down. *Colin Walker.*

Avro Anson LT830 of No.7 Air Gunnery School *R.A.F. Museum P9505*

Armstrong Whitworth Whitley Mk I & IV used for gunnery training. *R.A.F. Museum 5775-12*

Boulton & Paul Defiant. *R.A.F. Museum 5899-2*

German aircraft from above and fired a Very signal flare at it. The flare missed but it caused the pilot to take evasive action. However, the Ju 88's rear gunner fired at the Henley, damaging the port wing and forcing Wing Commander Jones to return to Stormy Down. Reference to this incident does not appear in the Station Record Book, possibly because it was felt judicious not to bring it to the attention of Group Headquarters!

Mr Geoff Arnold served as a wireless operator/air gunner with Bomber Command and was awarded the DFM and bar. He joined No 8 Air Gunnery course and still vividly remembers the roar of the Fairy Battles as they warmed up to carry the "dog-collared sprogs" to nearby Margam Sands for air to ground firing with the ancient Vickers gas operated guns. "I see myself being violently sick again as the pilot flies round and round the target area. "For God's sake, when are you going to fire?" he bellows down the intercom tube. In sheer desperation I put the gun over the side of the aircraft and hold my finger on the trigger. Back at the airfield I stagger white-faced from the aircraft. The pilot comes over to me, slaps me on the back and says "Good show, son. That's the best bit of shooting I've seen for a long time!"

Mr Almond agrees that the training was superficial but, nevertheless, it was effective because they were taught to fire straight, anticipating the movement of the enemy aircraft, rather than "hose-piping". He joined 102 Squadron at RAF Driffield when he left Stormy Down and fortunately found that there were few German fighters about during the early stages of the war, although the position changed considerably later.

The first fatal accidents were recorded on 11 February, 1940. With cloud at 1000 feet and whilst flying in snow showers, a Henley aircraft, L3339, piloted by Flying Officer J N Thornewill and with a passenger, Flying Officer J N Lemon, crashed on rocks at Rest Bay. Both men were killed. Just over fifty years later, in July 1991, two Coastguard Officers, John David and Byron Keylock discovered part of the wing structure from that aircraft washed up on Sker Beach.

On the same day, 11 February, a Wallace aircraft crashed on the Margam Ranges, killing Flying Officer C P S Smith and his passenger LAC L D Stratford.

The complement of aircraft located on the airfield had increased by 29 February,

Coastguard Officers John David & Byron Keylock with part of wing structure of 'Henley' L3339, which was washed up on Sker beach in July 1991.

John David

1940, to 14 Whitleys, 9 Battles, 9 Wallaces, 5 Harrows, 9 Henleys and 2 Magisters.

Considerable problems were being experienced in providing the required level of training for air gunners. In addition to the atrocious weather, which curtailed flying, a report on the outcome of No 7 Air gunnery course shows that there were no cannon guns available and that instruction was being given for them with the aid of notes. Turret manipulation was excluded because the 200 and 400 yard firing ranges was not operational and air exercises with camera guns could not be carried out because of a shortage of suitable aircraft. The unserviceability of the Whitley aircraft and shortage of suitable towing aircraft for the target drogues added to the difficulties. The slippery grass of the airfield, for there were no runways, lead to many accidents; one of the first was on 23 April 1940 when a Hampden bomber skidded and ran into a boundary hedge. Fortunately there were no injuries.

On 21 August, 1940, at 11.48 a.m., the Station suffered its only experience of enemy action. Three enemy aircraft, believed to be Junkers 88's, appeared from low cloud and before any warning could be given, dropped 11 bombs and fired their guns randomly towards the buildings. The bombs dropped into the Instructional Section, two striking the building housing the unit Post Office and some instructional equipment, and demolishing it. The postal clerk and another airman were killed. An adjacent building, in which an educational class was in progress, was demolished. The other bombs fell amongst buildings and caused little damage. In addition to the two airmen who were killed during the attack, fifteen were injured, five being detained in hospital. There was only a brief interruption to the training, however; by the next day the debris had been cleared and the school had returned to its normal routine.

There were nightly reports of enemy aircraft passing at high altitude over the airfield in a northerly direction throughout October, and there were a total of 60 alerts during the month.

On 1 November, 1940, the Station was re-named "R.A.F. Stormy Down", no reason being given for the overnight change of identity, but almost certainly it was to avoid confusion with R.A.F. Newton in Nottinghamshire. On the 12th of that month a hurricane, with a wind strength estimated at 100 m.p.h, damaged 3

Whitley bombers, 2 Wallaces and a Hind. One of the Whitleys cartwheeled access the airfield but fortunately missed all the other aircraft.

The lack of accommodation was causing problems and on 26 November Group Captain A W Franklyn drove down to Coney Beach to inspect the building that was being taken over as a billet for trainee Air Gunners and Air Observers. It is possible that this was one of the two 1914-18 aircraft hangars that had been erected on the site as part of the fun fair.

In December 1940, No 3 Ground Armament School opened at Stormy Down, providing training for Fitters and Fitter Armourers (later to be termed as Armourers). Many Naval Air Mechanics were also trained at the school, which remained at Stormy Down until January 1942, when it transferred to R.A.F. Kirkham.

Another fatal accident was reported on 4 March 1941. At 12.45 p.m, a Fairy Battle, L5019, piloted by Sergeant Pilot Tock and with two pupils from the No 30 Air Gunners Course, A/C Staunch and A/C Shepherd, was seen by the pilot of another Battle that was towing a target drogue to be turning steeply with white smoke or fumes pouring from the aircraft. The towing Battle tried to follow but the other aircraft, disappeared. Later the police telephoned the Station to report that a civilian had seen an aircraft crash into the sea off Porthcawl. No trace was found of the Battle or of its crew.

The following month, on 20 April 1941, a Battle, L5072, took off after the completion of repairs by the maintenance unit. It was piloted by Sergeant Dindorf and two fitters, AC1 Richardson and AC2 Elliot but shortly after take-off, at 4.40 p.m., it dived into the ground near Cern Cribbwr, killing all the occupants.

On 2 May, 1941, at 10.10 a.m., a Battle, 1211, towing a target drogue, crashed near the Kenfig Pool and burst into flames. The pilot, P/O Puklo and the drogue operator, AC2 Williams were killed.

A happier outcome resulted from the difficulty experienced by Pilot Officer Gardner, who was piloting Whitley, VT4163, accompanied by a rigger and four trainee air gunners. He took off on 15 June 1941 but shortly afterwards, at 4.20 p.m., the blade of the port airscrew snapped off, followed shortly afterwards by

Westland Wallace Two-Seat Biplane, used for Target Towing   R.A.F. Museum 5540-12

Westland Lysander. Two-seater aircraft used for Target Towing.   R.A.F. Museum 5852-4

58

the failure of the starboard engine. The aircraft was by then over the sea but it turned for shore and pancaked on sand-dunes near Sker Point. The starboard engine then burst into flames but whilst four of the crew managed to escape, Pilot Officer Gardner found himself trapped in the cockpit and one of the air gunners was lying unconscious in the front turret. The four who had escaped the wreck fought valiantly to rescue the two trapped men inspite of the risk of an imminent explosion and finally succeeded in rescuing them. Flight Sergeant Francis was awarded the British Empire Medal for the action he took during the rescue.

Unfortunately, the fatal accidents continued at Stormy Down. On 22 June a Fairy Battle, piloted by Flight Lieutenant Swann and with Pilot Officer Kitching as observer, hit the top of a tree on one of the farms of Margam Estate during a co-operation exercise with the Home Guard. The aircraft crashed and both were killed. On 31 August, at 4.50 p.m., another Battle, L5657, dived into the sea from 4000 ft, on a bearing of 255 degrees and five miles from Nash Point. The crew, Sergeant Naylor, LAC Bond and AC2 Sullivan, were never found.

The Fairy Battles became infamous for their unreliability and it must have been with great relief that pilots and trainees learned that they were being replaced with Lysanders. Eleven Lysanders arrived between 20th September and 12 October to be used as towing aircraft for the drogues. It was also announced that Defiants would be used to provide turret training for air gunners and nine of these aircraft arrived between 10 October and 4 December whilst a dual control Miles Master landed on 8 October to convert pilots to flying the Defiants.

In December 1941, 25 Group HQ, which was becoming extremely concerned about the effect that poor weather conditions were having on training, issued a directive that the war effort must be increased so that the fullest use be made of suitable weather to achieve maximum flying hours. Stormy Down adopted a seven day week programme, with 50% of the personnel being on duty on Saturdays or Sundays.

At the end of January, 1942, a Botha aircraft arrived for trials, with a view to it replacing the Whitley Marks 1-1V, which were not equipped with modern power-operated turrets and whose serviceability was continuously bad. After a week's trials it was decided that the Botha was not suitable for all the year flying unless concrete runways were built and that it would not help the proposed introduction of night flying in the Air Gunners' syllabus. A further five Defiants were added to the complement of the Station on 31 January.

Even the new aircraft were not immune from fatal crashes, however. On 8 February, 1942, a Defiant, N1761, piloted by Pilot Officer Read and with LAC Battle as crew, crashed on landing 200 yards from the south boundary of the airfield. It was suggested that this was due to the pilot not maintaining flying speed which caused the aircraft to spin in from a low height. The pilot was killed and LAC Battle was injured.

On 12 February a Lysander, P1719, crashed 800 yards north east of Kenfig Hill. The pilot, Sergeant Roffey, and AC1 Thomas were both killed, the former being buried in Nottage cemetery. A happier fate was enjoyed by the crew of Lysander V9786, which crashed into the sea and sank at 12.50 p.m., on 9 March 1942. Both the pilot, Flight Sergeant Hoare, and AC1 Nelson were picked up by H.M. Mine sweeper "Fairfax".

On 8 April 1942 a tragic accident killed a young ATS girl, Private Lydia Amy Slingo, as she was standing outside a cook house with ATS Corporal Eva Winifred Taylor and an Army Bombadier. The cook house is believed to have stood in the area now occupied by Hutchwyns Close. Private Slingo was hit and killed by a bullet fired from a Whitley bomber, K8942. Corporal Taylor told the Inquest, which was held in the Seabank Hotel, that she had just left the cook house when they heard an aircraft passing overhead. "I heard machine-gun fire", she said, "and almost immediately something flashed passed my face". Private Slingo put her hand to her shoulder. "Something has hit me", she said, and almost immediately she rolled over and was caught by the Bombadier. She died immediately. The post-mortem showed that a bullet had entered behind her right shoulder and had taken a downward course, striking the upper surface of the fifth rib which was then fractured. It then took a course at right angles, piercing the right lung, heart and left lung.

The inquest heard that the Whitley bomber was carrying six Air Gunner pupils under the command of Gunnery Instructor Sergeant W J Dawson. The pilot, Sergeant J B Denton, told the court that he was flying the aircraft to the firing ranges out at sea and as he was crossing the coast one of the pupils, Sergeant Bent Joseph Hardesty of the Royal Canadian Air Force, whose home was in Winnepeg, had fired from the front turret without authority. The usual method of giving clearance for firing was for the pilot to give the thumbs up to the Instructor, who stood or crouched at the entrance to the nose, and he then tapped the pupil on the shoulder, indicating when it was safe to fire. Sergeant Hardesty admitted that he had fired a burst when he thought the aircraft was going out to sea and explained that there had been a stoppage in the gun and that he thought it would be safe to clear it. The Coroner told the jury that they would wish to take into account Sergeant Hardesty's record; although he was acting contrary to instructions, he seemed to have done what he did out of enthusiasm for his work. A verdict of "accidental death" was returned.

Mr Jack Winchester, who was a Flight Sergeant at Stormy Down and was in charge of the airmen who operated the towing drogues, remembered an accident that possibly should never have happened. A 21 year old Polish pilot, Sergeant Bluczynski, had attracted his attention because of the latter's affection for low flying. On 14 April, 1942, Flight Sergeant Winchester drew the Polish pilot to one side and told him that he could fly as he liked when he was alone but that whilst he was carrying airmen he was not to put their lives at risk. The following day Sergeant Bluczynski, with AC1 Hocknell as the drogue operator behind him, dived beneath high tension cables and crashed. Sergeant Bluczynski now lies in Nottage cemetery.

Whitley aircraft were used to give Porthcawl's Air Training Corps the experience of flying in June 1942.

On 19 July 1942, the early bird risers amongst Porthcawl's residents would have seen a combined civil and military exercise, simulating the effects of an invasion and attack on Porthcawl. Simulation exercise began at 5.40 a.m and possibly because the organisers felt it unlikely that more than a handful of the town's residents would have been up and about at such an hour, 30 members of the Women's Auxiliary Air Force (W.A.A.F), who were billeted in the R.A.F. Marine Base in Jennings Building, took the role of panic-stricken civilians. Two Defiants carried out (simulated) dive-bombing attacks and street fighting went on all morning.

By August 1942,The Defiant aircraft had been fitted with camera guns and were being used for air gunnery practice. They also carried out simulated dive-bombing attacks over Dan-y-graig with No 9 A.A. Royal Artillery unit and over

Margan with the local Home Guard.

On 18 August, 1942, the body of 69876/105 Unter Offizier Walter Knoppik, aged 22, of the Luftwaffe was washed up on Newton Beach. He had been the pilot of a Heinkel He 111 of 8/KG 53 which had bombed Swansea on the night of August 4/5. A Beaufighter of 215 Squadron, based at Fairwood Common, shot the Heinkel down off Ilfracombe. Unter Offizier Knoppick was buried in Nottage cemetery on 21 August 1942 with full military honours. In April, 1963, his body was taken to the German War Cemetery at Cannock Chase.

Although it was summer the Station was suffering major problems in carrying out the training programme because of persistent bad weather, featuring storms and poor visibility, and also because of convoys in the Bristol Channel were making it impossible to use the firing ranges for long periods.

Another fatal crash occurred on 22 September 1942, when at 5.45 p.m. a Defiant, T4075, towing a target drogue, dived into the sea 1/2 mile off Port Talbot. The body of the New Zealand pilot, Flight Sergeant Shrimpton, RNZAF, was later found near Ogmore and that of Sergeant Teskey was washed ashore at Taibach Beach, Port Talbot. Both were buried in Nottage cemetery.

The condition of the grass landing area at R.A.F. Stormy Down was causing difficulties and was the cause of damage to aircraft. On 4 February, 1943, the operations record book refers to considerable damage to Lysander T1558 caused by ground subsidence under the starboard undercarriage unit. The report states that "This airfield is subject to these subsidences due to broken rock under its surface, allowing water to collect and overflow after heavy and continuous rain, thus washing earth away with it and creating heavy cavities, causing airfield surface to cave in when a heavy weight is brought to bear on top".
As if to underline the complaint, on 3 March, 1943, a Whitley aircraft made a normal landing but during taxiing the wheels sank up to the axles into hidden subsidence.

The weather was fine and clear after a misty start, however, for the Station to support Porthcawl's "Wings for Victory" Week on 27 March, 1943. Timed to coincide with the opening ceremony, a fly-past took place at 5 p.m. four formations of nine Whitleys and the same number of Defiants and Lysanders. A total of

£80,000 was raised during the week.

A decision had been taken to replace the Lysanders for target towing duties and the first Martinet arrived on 21 April 1943. It had also been decided that Avro Ansons should replace the Whitleys and two Ansons arrived on 25 May. On 30 May one of these was scrambled when a report was received that an enemy submarine had been sighted 6 miles west of Scarweather Lightship; the Anson searched for an hour but could not find any trace of the submarine.

On 2 July 1943, it was announced that "effective today Whitley aircraft cease to operate on Air Gunnery programmes". By 13 July the Station had 18 Martinets and there were still 16 Lysanders which were being replaced.

On 21 September, at 2.35 p.m., an Anson, LT88, piloted by a Polish pilot, Sergeant Strycharek, flying with an Instructor and 3 U/T Air gunners, collided at 600 feet with a Lysander T1588, carrying Sergeant Routledge and AC R Tarling. Both aircraft crashed, killing the occupants, one quarter of a mile NNW of the Stormy Down Airfield Boundary. They were buried at Nottage on 27 September 1943.

Units of a United States Infantry Division had moved into Porthcawl in preparation for the invasion of Europe and two U.S. Army Air Corps "Piper Cub" aircraft were attached to Stormy Down for housing and maintenance purposes on 8 November. They operated from a landing ground adjacent to West Drive, Porthcawl and belonged to the 107th Artillery Battalion.

On 5 January 1944 two Wellington bombers landed at R.A.F. Stormy Down for Air Gunnery trials, to see if they were more efficient than Ansons. They left on 13 January to test landings on the concrete runways at Llandow, foreshadowing the end of Stormy Down as an airfield some months later.

On 13 January, in fair weather, one of the new Martinets, MS525, piloted by Flight Sergeant J Ruddell (RCAF), flew into a mountain two miles north-east of Port Talbot. He was buried in Nottage on 31 January 1944, but his gravestone records that his rank was Pilot Officer.

It was reported on 8 February, 1944 that "In consequence of the very bad state of

R.A.F. Museum 5904-5

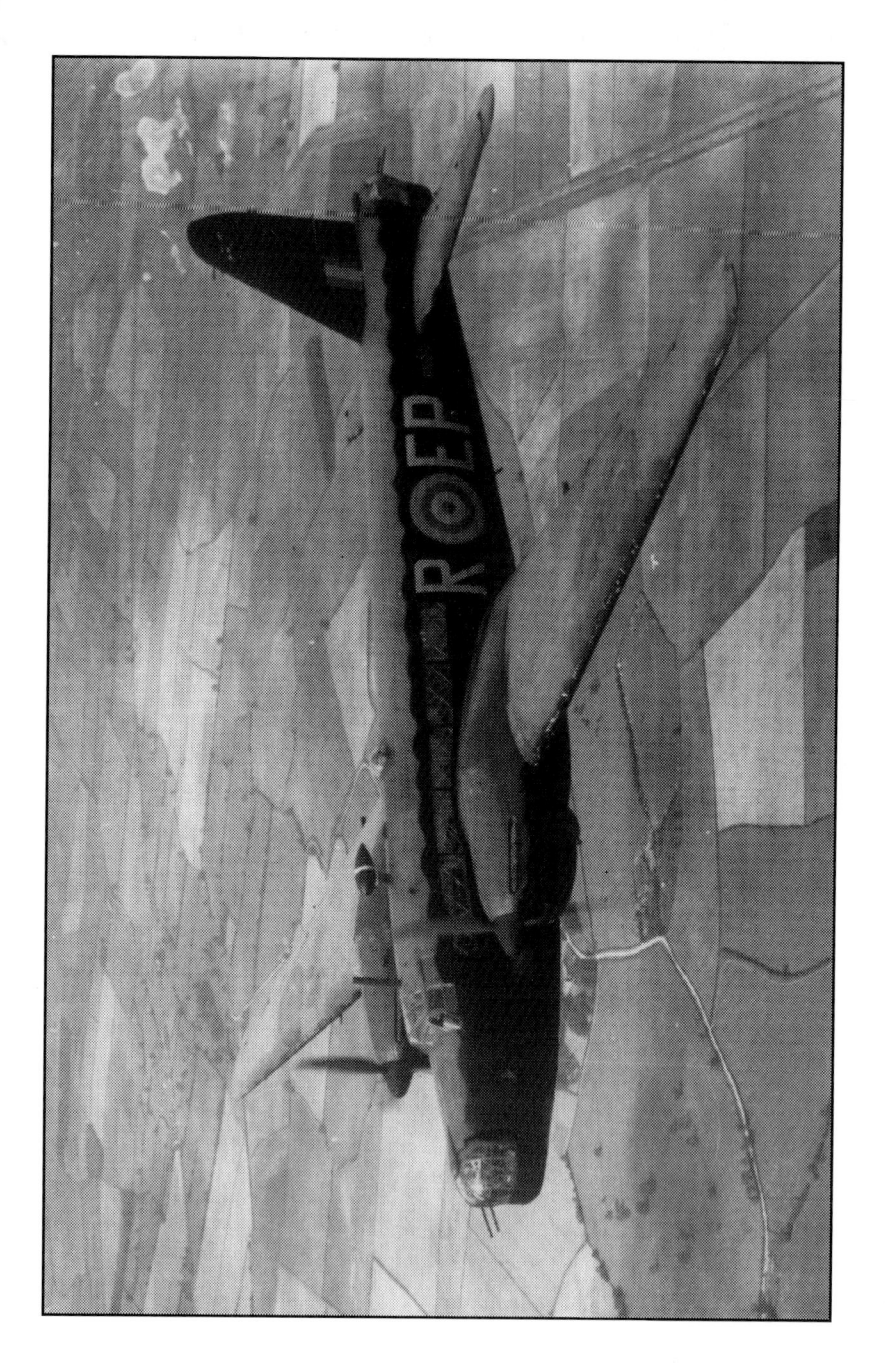

Vickers Wellington II

64

the airfield requiring considerable reconstruction and repair, Rhoose airfield will be taken over as a satellite of Stormy Down for a provisional period of six months in order that Air Gunnery training commitments can be fulfilled". 23 Ansons and 20 Martinets, together with 50 pilots were despatched to the satellite station and it was decreed that Stormy Down airfield would be kept open for visitors and for ferrying aircraft to and from Rhoose for minor inspections and repairs.

Further developments were occurring which would lead to the cessation of flying from Stormy Down; on 28 February it was announced that the detached Martinet towing flight that had been operating with a Wellington on turret training trials at R.A.F. Llandow had been satisfactorily completed.

On 27 March 1944 a Martinet, EM456, piloted by Flight Sergeant Westmorland and accompanied by tow target operator LAC Reed, dived straight into the sea 14 miles and 200 degrees off Porthcawl. The aircraft sank in 14 fathoms and no trace was found of the occupants. Divers were sent down to examine the wreckage and found that it had been holed by 20mm cannon shell and it was thought that the Martinet had been mistaken for a German plane and had been shot down by allied guns, possibly by a Typhoon fighter aircraft.

A horrific accident was seen by many Porthcawl residents on 8 May 1944 when two Ansons, LV300 and MG131 collided whilst flying in formation on a cine gun exercise with a third Anson and a Martinet attack aircraft near Porthcawl. Both aircraft sank 1 1/4 miles from Porthcawl Point on a bearing of 275 degrees true. Recovery of the bodies of the two crews took from 1 June until 10 July. Those killed were:-

Anson MG131
Pilot F/Sgt Deans
    AC2 Holland
    AC2 Kelman

Anson LV300
Pilot F/Sgt Davis *(RCAF)*
    Buried Nottage
    AC2 Robinson
    AC2 Knowles
    AC2 Shoesmith
    AC2 Grisenthwaite

On 10 May, 1944, No W68 Elementary Gliding School commenced ATC Glider

Training from the airfield.

On 21 August 1944 all No 7 Air Gunnery School pilots, tow-target operators and Flying Control staff were posted to other units in 25 Group following the disbandment of the flying activities at Stormy Down. A signal was sent to the Air Ministry that "no further flying facilities exist at the Station". The problems of unstable ground and a dangerously slippery grass landing strip had made it impracticable for the heavier aircraft that were now in service to use the airfield and far better facilities existed at Llandow.

Although flying training may have ended, this was by no means the end of the Stormy Down story.

On 12 August 1944 W/Cdr Moxham, A.F.C., accompanied by W/Cdr Ashman, Senior Education Officer, visited Stormy Down for discussions with officers representing 54 Group and 25 Group. These discussions were in connection with the transfer of No 40 Initial Training Wing to Stormy Down and on 1 September the first u/t pilots and flight engineers arrived at the Station. By 29 October, 142 u/t engineers and 382 pilots had been accommodated. However, the occupation by 40 ITW was short lived. On 8 November the personnel enjoyed an Ensa concert in the Station's "Turret" cinema. On 22 November, 430 cadets, 23 officers and 9 NCOs boarded a special train from Pyle and were posted to RAF Bridgenorth and between 25th and 27th of that month a further 151 pilots moved out. On 27 November 1944 it was announced that 40 Initial Training Wing had been disbanded.

The departure of 40 ITW did not lead to a quiet life at Stormy Down, however. On 26 November No. 23 (French) Initial Training Wing left R.A.F. Filey at 5 p.m. and arrived at Pyle Railway Station at 8 a.m. on the following day. The Wing consisted of Free French trainee pilots, navigators, bomb-aimers, wireless operators, flight engineers, and air gunners.

They were given little opportunity to recover from their journey; on 7 December the Central Examination Board tested all the trainees and a high proportion failed. A Board of Officers was assembled to discover the reason and put the failure rate down to the disruption caused by the transfer from Filey. A further examination was carried out in early January, 1945, when 38 out of the 77 cadets failed and were re-flighted for further training. Significantly better results were achieved in further examinations at the end of the month.

Staff and trainees were, however, suffering because of difficulties in the heating system which was the subject of investigation. There was concern that the comfort of the personnel was being impaired and as a temporary measure, supplementary heating was being provided by oil lamps.

Provision of entertainment was also a priority in order to maintain the morale of the service men and women. Ensa again visited the Station on 6 December 1944 and provided the personnel with a first class variety concert. A gramaphone club was organised, providing music "of a classical nature", and a good attendance was noted. On 11 December, the Recreational and Reference Libraries were reopened.
A "Ralph Reader Gang Show" visited the Station on 13 December and provided an excellent concert, the cast subsequently being entertained in the Sergeants' Mess.

Arrangements had been made with the Overseas Club whereby the hospitality of many families living in the vicinity of the Station was extended to foreign personnel serving at Stormy Down. British and overseas servicemen and women were welcomed into the homes of Porthcawl's residents and this was especially appreciated by the French airmen and by those British personnel who were unable to get home at weekends. A good understanding had also been achieved with the local transport authorities and bus company, who appreciated the problems of personnel in such an isolated location.

A traditional Christmas Day Dinner was served in the Messes and films were shown in the afternoon in the camp cinema. The French held their own concert in the Station NAAFI. The weather was particularly harsh, with prolonged frost and there were several burst pipes to add to the discomfort of those who were unable to spend Christmas at home. On Boxing Day there was a Station Dance in the NAAFI, a party for the cooks in the Airman's Mess and a competition for the huts with the best Christmas decorations in the WAAFs section. On 2 January 1945 103 Flight Engineers and Air Gunners took their final examinations and on 4 January the French servicemen gave a Variety concert for the whole station in the cinema to a "large and appreciative audience".

The numbers of personnel at RAF Stormy Down varied throughout the months, but on 31 January 1945 it totalled 985 and consisted of:

PERMANENT STAFF: 55 Officers, 59 SNCOs, 132 Corporals and Aircraftmen, 5 WAAF Officers 6 WAAF SNCOs and 191 WAAF Corporals and Aircraftwomen.

FRENCH AIR FORCE: 6 Permanent Staff Officers, 29 Cadet Officers, 30 Permanent Staff SNCOs, 183 Cadet SNCOs, 51 Corporals and Aircraftmen and 238 cadet corporals and aircraftmen.

The well ordered routine of the Station was interrupted at 5 a.m. on Sunday, 11 March, 1945 with a telephone call from the police. There had been mass escape at about 10 p.m the previous evening of 67 German prisoners of war from their camp at Island Farm, Bridgend, and the Royal Air Force was requested to help in their recapture. By 0630 a.m. all outer posts had been manned and instructions had been given to the armed servicemen to stop all vehicles and check identities. If there were any doubts, the individuals were to be detained and the police called. Anyone failing to stop when clearly called on to do so "was to be fired on (in the legs)". It was not explained how this was to be achieved in the case of a car speeding past a roadblock!

During the morning four search parties of French officers, NCOs, cadets and other ranks set out enthusiastically to comb allocated areas west and south of the aerodrome, and in the afternoon a further four parties, each seventy strong, scoured the area. No prisoners were found.

At 3 p.m., police at Bridgend phoned to say that 10 Prisoners of War had been seen at Laleston and as large a search party as possible was asked for. A total of 57 French Air force personnel was hastily assembled and divided into groups, each under a British officer and allocated to various very wooded and boggy areas. One of these groups captured 5 escaped Germans. At 10.15 p.m that night a picket mounting guard at one of the outer cordon posts saw four Germans and captured them A short time later, at 11 p.m, two French servicemen spotted two POW escapees; one kept watch whilst the other called the police and both Germans were recaptured.

The search continued on 12 March, with a report that there had been an attempted break-in at a farmhouse 5 miles NNW of the Station. A 60 strong party was sent out at 10 a.m, but the area was very wooded and no fugitives were found. A similar message regarding the same farmhouse was received on 13 March and another search party was sent out, but again, without success. On 17 March the Station was informed that all the prisoners had been recaptured.

In their off-duty hours the French trainee aircrew were taken on visits to factories, such as the Nickel Company, the National Oil Refinery (now B.P.) at Baglan, a colliery and a steel mill. There was close liasion with civilian organisations in Swansea and numbers of French officers and NCOs stayed with families for periods extending from weekends to the full period of their ten days leave. Trips were organised by sea to Liverpool and to Glasgow and there were many fishing trips.

In April 1945, however, it was necessary for the Station Commander and the Adjutant to visit Porthcawl Urban District Council in order to ask for measures to be taken to prevent service personnel being evicted from their bed & breakfast accommodation in order to make room for summer visitors. The Council gave an assurance that every effort would be made "to stop this insidious practice".

On 30 April, as a change of scene, the regular Station Dance was held in the Grand Pavilion, where it was declared to be very successful if almost too crowded!

Porthcawl celebrated VE (Victory in Europe) day on 5 May 1945 with an impressive parade which included contingent's of the RAF, the WAAF and the Free French Air Force. On May 25 RAF personnel from Stormy Down produced a revue, "Slipstream", in the Grand Pavilion.

The numerical strength of the mainly French complement of the Station continued to grow; it had risen to 1218 by the end of May and by the end of June it totalled 1468.

Bastille Day, 14 July 1945 was celebrated by the Free French with a march through Porthcawl. All the French personnel took part, together with one flight of RAF servicemen and one flight from the WAAF unit. In the evening a dance was organised at Stormy Down and the Royal Ordnance Factory at Bridgend provided a spectacular firework display.

On Tuesday night, 28 August 1945, clashes occurred between the Free French servicemen and civilians. The trouble began on the Monday night over a dispute involving a woman. The following night a contingent of about 100 Free Frenchmen walked out of Stormy Down without permission and assembled on the Promenade. Running flights broke out between the Frenchmen and the civilians and police reinforcements were called up from Bridgend, Port Talbot and Maesteg. The RAF and the West Yorkshire Regiment were also called upon to help but the trouble ended with the arrival of police reinforcements and Free French Officers successfully ordered their men back to Stormy Down. It was reported that one Frenchmen was injured in the neck and that an RAF man had to have medical treatment.

On 31 August, a 22 year old collier of Newton-Nottage, Porthcawl, was sent to prison for two months with hard labour for using threatening behaviour on the seafront. The evidence against him was that he had been at the centre of a group of Free Frenchmen and had seemed to be doing his best to stir up trouble between them and British soldiers. He was heard to call out "It's no use speaking to these French *******. They can't understand ******* English. What the hell are they doing here, anyway?" He was arrested, partly for his own safety, but also for causing a breach of the peace.

Good relations were soon restored and just before Christmas there was a party for the children of the RAF families and fifty orphans from Porthcawl and Bridgend were invited. The meal consisted of Creme of Victory soup, followed by roast turkey, ham and sausage seasoning, roast pork, creamed and roast potatoes, sprouts and peas, with Christmas pudding in whisky sauce and mince pies to follow. This was a luxurious meal for those times, when rationing restricted the amount and variety of food.

On 21 February 1946 a special parade of the French took place, with the Station Commander taking the salute. In the evening there was a farewell dance in the NAAFI and on 23 February, 279 French officers and men left for France, followed by a further 279 on 28 February. There were farewell dances for the RAF personnel in the Officers' and Sergeants' Messes during March and on 4 April

1946 there was a ceremonial colour-lowering parade. The remaining French moved to Bridgenorth and on 21 April the Station Commander moved to RAF Market Harborough.

RAF Stormy Down was placed on a care and maintenance basis, with only No 68 Gliding School remaining for the Air Training Corps, until it was moved to RAF St Athan in March 1947. In October 1948 Stormy Down became a surplus inactive station parented by St. Athan.

Some of the huts were used as accommodation for workers building the new steel works at Port Talbot and in 1948 the Steel Company converted the gymnasium into a cinema, which was open to the general public until it closed in 1953. Most of the hangars were dismantled and in 1951 one of them was moved to Cardiff and became the Sophia Gardens Pavilion. It collapsed in January 1982 after a very heavy snowfall. In the 1960's some of the buildings were used by the Home Office and Women's Royal Voluntary Service for their stores and part of the airfield was used by the Porthcawl Gliding Club. Most of the huts disappeared as the quarry expanded almost up to the married quarters but the Station's sick quarters and main stores were used until 1993 as a Department of Social Security Resettlement Centre. When the Centre closed all the buildings were demolished.

The expansion of the quarry caused the road that runs through the camp to be diverted to the east and it now runs past the harmonisation range which is used by the Territorial Army. The remaining buildings were sold to a private owner in 1986 and are used as an indoor Go-Kart track and Sunday market.

During its operational life more than 7000 air gunners were trained at RAF Stormy Down, as well as some 400 Air Observers, whilst approximately 2000 Flight Engineers, in training at RAF St Athan, did a short ground gunnery course there. In addition to the 10,000 aircrew who passed through the school a considerable number of pilots, many of them from the Fleet Air Arm, underwent armament training before qualifying for their wings.

The aerodrome played a significant part in providing trained aircrew for the squadrons of Lancasters and other aircraft that carried out devastating attacks on Nazi Germany. The men who served there also brought a great deal exuberance to Porthcawl and much pleasure to the young women who attended the Station dances or who were in demand in the Grand Pavilion. Perhaps the best epitaph is that given by ex-Flight Sergeant Jack Winchester : "Many hundreds of navigators and air gunners passed through Stormy Down on their way to Bomber and Coastal Commands - many, unfortunately, never to see the end of the war. There were also all the non-flying airmen and WAAFs, the fitters, riggers, electricians, armourers, parachute packers, etc who all did their bit towards the war effort. Every person stationed at Stormy Down during those war years would agree that it was a happy aerodrome and the local inhabitants made us so welcome. Many of us met local young ladies and settled into the family life of Porthcawl and a few, like myself, are still here 50 years later".

CHAPTER SIX

RAF AIR SEA RESCUE, MARINE CRAFT UNIT, PORTHCAWL

An Air Sea Rescue Unit was operating form Porthcawl's outer harbour from the early days of the war, using the century old stone building, Jennings Warehouse and during this time the slipway was significantly improved to enable marine craft to be drawn up for servicing. At any one time two 37 ft boats were stationed in the harbour, and ASRs 274, 282, 283, 294 and 295 have been recorded as operating from the base for varying periods from September 1939 until August 1940. On 4 November 1939 two ASR boats were called out to trawl for a German mine, which they found and successfully beached at Port Talbot. In August, 1940, the S.S "Stalheim:, a 719 ton Norwegian freighter hit a mine off Port Talbot and the crew were rescued by ASR 274. The Unit was disbanded for a short period but on 21 August, 1941 a letter was sent from Headquarters Flying Training Command to RAF Stormy Down stating that the Air Sea Rescue service was being considerably expanded and that a new section would be located at Porthcawl. It would be operationally controlled by 19 Group and attached as a lodger unit to Stormy Down for administration. The section was given the title of No 46 Air Sea Rescue Marine Craft Unit.

The unit was again housed in Jennings Warehouse, which offered ideal accommodation for living and sleeping accommodation for the crew and servicing personnel and also adequate space for servicing boats under cover. By November 1941 two 41 ft seaplane tenders (436 and 437) had been allocated to the unit and a section of two corporals and six airmen had been formed.

During November and December 1941, however, there was correspondence between RAF Stormy Down and HQ Flying Training Command regarding the responsibility for the operational control of the marine craft. On 3 January 1942 an officer from 19 Group visited the unit and undertook to forward detailed instructions regarding the administration of the unit. In the meantime, the operational control would be vested in the appropriate Naval authority, which had to be informed on all occasions when the boats were sent out on rescue operations. Close liaison was to be maintained with the Resident Naval Officer at Porthcawl, Commander Rudolf Burmester.

ASR 283 at buoy off Porthcawl, 1940.

John David

John David

No. 282 on slipway, January, 1940.

Stormy Down then pressed that the selection of Porthcawl as a base for Air Sea Rescue craft should be reviewed, because in rough weather boats on stand-by could not be tied up to their buoys in the Bristol Channel and could not be moored in the tidal harbour from two hours before and two hours after low water. Coastal Command gave short shrift to this suggestion; the excellent maintenance facilities at Porthcawl made it an ideal location. However, in deference to the problems of mooring in the Channel in bad weather, the buoys would be moved closer in towards the Pier to give greater protection.

In May, 1942, the new Resident Naval Officer in Porthcawl, Commander Hugh Pritchard, issued his instructions on the use of the boats. In emergency, every effort was to be made to despatch a launch in the shortest possible time. The RNO's directions were to be obtained for any movements other than emergency. In daylight hours a launch must always be afloat and ready and if the boat was moored in the Channel, sufficient crew for movement must be aboard. Between sunset to sunrise the launch was not to remain at the off-shore buoy; this was later rescinded to allow the launch to remain outside the harbour in acceptable conditions. The skiff used by RAF crews to ferry to and from the launch could not be taken beyond the Pier head except in conditions of smooth water. In the absence of the RNO, the Station Officer, Porthcawl Coastguard would be responsible. Finally, the boats could only use a prescribed area, between Newton Point and Fairy Buoy for testing engines.

The new crews settled into routine of an operational unit, varying between practice runs in the "prescribed areas" and occasional calls for assistance; between 9 November 1941 and 30 September 1943 it was recorded that they answered 25 emergency calls. In November 1943 Porthcawl lost its Resident Naval Officer and the RNO at Barry took over responsibility. In that month Lunch 437, one of the original pair assigned to Porthcawl in 1941, was taken up the slipway and found to be badly damaged on the port side of the hull. She was made seaworthy and set out for Ferryside where there were facilities for repairs to the hull. Both engines failed shortly after leaving the harbour and the launch was finally towed in by a pinnace from the marine base at Barry, which fortunately happened to be passing enroute for Ferryside.

One ex-airman who remembers the time he spent at the Marine Base between February and July 1943 is Mr Mike Flynn, who now lives in Sheffield. Mr Flynn had initially been posted as a groundcrew wireless operator from RAF Compton Bassett to Stormy Down, where he was billeted in a hut facing the Bridgend - Pyle Road - conveniently close to a gap in the hedge which enabled him to slip in and out of camp without a pass. On the morning after returning from a week's unofficial "holiday", he and another airman, A/C Gendle, were told to report immediately to the Marine Base. The two newly assigned boat crewmen took turns at cooking the meals on the boat, which the regular hands insisted should be oily and greasy, a menu that, until they acquired their sea-legs, did not help their ability to hold down their food.

"There was not a great deal of action at that time", Mr Flynn recalls "and we spent our time at sea fishing and sunbathing. We did have the company of six WAAFs from Stormy Down who would come down when they were off duty and change in the wireless room. We would all swim in the harbour and sunbathe. Afterwards we ran a shuttle service with two bikes to get them back to camp. One or two girls would ride on the crossbar and we'd carry them two miles or so and then they'd wait whilst we rode back for the others. Then we'd all walk the rest of the way to the camp entrance and then bicycle back to the marine base". It wasn't all just sunbathing and swimming, however. On one occasion Mr Flynn recalls the boat being called out on an emergency shout in very rough weather. "I was in the cabin with Flight Sergeant Ambler and was on the point of suggesting that we ought to turn back for safety's sake when he said that he didn't think that it would be safe to turn back. The waves were rising 25 - 30 feet above the boat. He decided to let the boat ride up on the wave and when it reached the peak, put on full power and turn. The manoeuvre worked, fortunately, but it was a very frightening experience".

On 2 October, 1943, a crash call was responded to by one of the boats on the report that a Lancaster, E110, from 619 Squadron had ditched off Llantwit Major whilst returning from a bombing raid and on the 4th October ST437 set out in heavy seas to search off Scarweather lightship for three airmen.
On 11 December 1943 an emergency call was received regarding an Anson which had crashed into the sea near Scarweather Sands. Launch ST436 was despatched but was informed after searching that the crew had been picked up by a dredger from Swansea. On its return from searching, however, 436 encountered heavy seas and the wheel-house was damaged, necessitating it being sent to Ferryside for repairs. Since Launch ST437 was also out of service, ST 1574 was delivered

by road as a replacement on 14 December, but by 1 January Stormy Down was complaining to HQ 19 Group that the tender was unsuitable for duty at Porthcawl. Experience had shown that on several occasions it had been unable to withstand the severity of the weather, especially when lying at the outer moorings. With a beam of only 8' - 9' and a confined deck space, picking up the outer moorings even in a moderate sea was a hazardous operation and in rough weather and during darkness it was extremely dangerous. A more seaworthy craft, suitable for local conditions, was requested.

The reply of 7 January was not particularly helpful; no tenders were available for replacement, although it was appreciated that the outer moorings were untenable in adverse weather.

Jennings Warehouse had been providing accommodation for NCOs and airmen at the No 7 Gunnery School at Stormy Down, but on 18 February 1944 they moved back to the Station.

On 12 April, 1944, an American soldier and his girlfriend, Hilda Cull, were walking along the breakwater when a huge wave swept them into the sea. This was seen by one of the aircraftmen at the Unit, AC Westhorp, who sounded the alarm and two LACs, George Ash and Derek Shackel rowed out in a dinghy. They recovered the body of Miss Cull but they could find no trace of the American, whose body was washed up at Newton the next day. LACs Ash and Shackel both received letters of appreciation from the RNLI and awards of £1 each.

A crash call on 8 May 1944 was for the two Ansons LV300 and MG131 which had crashed following a collision off Porthcawl Point. An empty dinghy and wreckage were taken on board but no survivors or bodies were found. Between 9 and 18 May an American Navy Diving unit tried to recover the bodies of the trapped airmen, without success. Their bodies began to be washed up at various points along the coast from 1 June.

On 15 September 1944 the Porthcawl Coastguard requested the duty boat to stand by U.S. Steamtug 672, U.S. Navy, which had run aground on Tusker Rocks whilst towing a U.S. Motor Towing Launch MTL 660. ST 437 went alongside the Steamtug, but the crew insisted on remaining aboard and the ASR launch returned to the outer mooring with the U.S. MTL 660 at 11 a.m. At 11.50 a.m. the Coastguard asked that the Coxswain of MTL 660 be brought ashore for interroga-

MTL 660 washed ashore at Trecco Bay, 15th September, 1944.

Bert Hayward

tion. The dinghy carrying the coxswain was unable to reach the pier because of a strong south-westerly wind and it was swept ashore at Coney Beach and brought round later to the pier. At 2.55 p.m the dinghy set off back to the ASR launch with LAC Shackel and LAC Rees but at 3 p.m it was struck by heavy seas and capsized. ST 437 tried to reach the airmen but was unable to get close enough to effect a rescue. LAC Shackel swam ashore but LAC Rees drowned and was later washed ashore at Coney Beach.

The position of the U.S. Steamtug 672 was worsening as the waves pounded her against the rocks. MTL 660 slipped her mooring to go to assist, but its engine failed and it was swept ashore at Trecco Bay. The Mumbles Lifeboat was called up to give assistance but the Tug was stuck on the rocks and finally capsized, with the loss of all five crew members. The anchor in front of the Pirates' Club is believed to be from the Steamtug.

On 21 September the U.S. Salvage Tug "Robert Emery" arrived off Tusker Rock with another MTL, No 816, with the intention of salvaging the grounded tug. The next day, at 6.35 p.m, ASR Launch ST 437 was called by the Coastguard to go to the assistance of MTL 816, which was dragging its anchor 1000 yards from Tusker Rock. The sea was very rough but the RAF launch succeeded in getting in line aboard the MTL and started towing it towards Porthcawl. Fifteen minutes later the MTL was able to proceed under its own power.

There was a period of calm for a month before the U.S. Navy brought a fresh excitement to Porthcawl. On 22 October, as MTL 816 was entering the Harbour, the engine room caught fire and the crew promptly abandoned ship. The "resting" ASR Launch was quickly removed to outer moorings, where it remained overnight. Porthcawl's National Fire Service was called into action and the fire was eventually extinguished at 9.30 p.m, but the fire crew remained throughout the night in case of further trouble. A U.S. tug arrived on 25 October to remove the damaged vessel.

An Anson, Number MG112, force-landed near Scarweather Sands on 11 December 1944 and ST 436 responded to the call-out. The seas were extremely heavy and the wheelhouse was damaged. Fortunately the crew of the Anson were rescued by a dredger from Swansea. The crew of a USAAF Marauder were also lucky when their aircraft force-landed off Margam. The duty ASR boat went to

Air Sea Rescue launches 443, 1512 & 1593 moored in Porthcawl harbour. Photograph taken in 1954.

John David

their rescue but the aircraft was close enough to the beach for the crew members to be able to wade ashore without help.

No further crash calls were reported until 23 July 1945 when a report was received that a Spitfire had crashed in the sea off the Margam bombing range. ST436 left in heavy seas and searched the area but could not find any trace of a crash and returned to base. Later that night the Coastguard reported that the body of a pilot had been recovered from submerged wreckage 1 1/2 miles from the Kenfig River. On 25 July ST 436 was called out again to the Margam bombing range on the report of a crashed Spitfire. This time oil was found and traces of wreckage. Ominously an airman's sock was found floating on the water.

Although the war was over, the Marine Base continued as an active Unit for nearly 14 more years. In March 1946 it became 1105 Marine Craft Unit and in 1951 it was equipped with two brand new launches, Nos 1593 and 1513. These spent much of their time at Watchet, towing targets for No 1 Air Gunnery School, based at R A F Watchet.

The first crash call recorded was on 4 March 1954 when ST 1593 went to the aid of a Vampire that had crashed in the sea off Ilfracombe. Sadly the pilot was dead when they reached him. On 20 April 1954, ST 1593 was called out to help boys cut off by the tide at Southerndown and on 23 May it was back at Southerndown rescuing a boy who had fallen over the cliffs.

By 1956 the Launches stationed at Porthcawl were RSL (Range Safety Launch) 1512 and 1593. RSL 443 was also there but was probably unserviceable. The launches were performing Range Safety Boat duties off Foreland Point and were also attending the Air to Air Firing Range used by RAF Chivenor as well as that at Pembrey. On 21 October a search was made for a crashed Javelin off Weston-Super-Mare; the wreckage was found and towed to Avonmouth.

On 9 August 1956 Range Safety Launch 1658 arrived from Blackmore's Yard at Bideford on allocation and on 17 August RSL 1512 towed 443 to Swansea Docks, where it was loaded on to a lorry and taken to Calshott. The crew of RSL 1512 rescued a young girl from the sea off Porthcawl beach on 22 August. At first she appeared to be dead but she was saved after artificial respiration.

RSL 1593 was sold by the Director of Naval Contracts on 11 March 1957 and on 5 April RSL 1657 arrived on allocation. On 21 June 1957, RSL 1512 was handed over to C H Bailey of Barry for sale. This left RSLs 1657 and 1658 operating from Porthcawl and the following year mention is also made of RSL 1643.

By January 1959 the boats were RSLs Nos 1657 and 1658. On 30 January a policy statement confirmed that 1105 Marine Craft Unit was established with 3 forty-three feet Range Safety Launches and one powered dinghy. One of these, RSL 1643, had been returned to 238 MU at Calshott and had not been replaced so there were effectively only two boats on station. The primary task was Search and Rescue, with a secondary task of Range Safety for RAF Chivenor. It was noted that the craft moored in Porthcawl harbour were subject to tidal conditions which restricted operations during inclement weather. Personnel were accommodated on the unit in Jennings building and a duty Search and Rescue crew could be available at fifteen minutes notice. The complement of the Unit was: 2 Flight Lieutenants, 2 Flight Sergeants, 6 Sergeants and 41 Airmen.

The launches were sailing regularly on Range Safety Duties and frequent helicopter exercises had taken place with 22 Squadron. These exercises may well have demonstrated that helicopters were far quicker and possibly more efficient at Search & Rescue than Marine Craft because only one month later, on 23 February 1959, the Colour was finally lowered at 8.30 a.m and without any other ceremony the RAF launches sailed away. In point of fact, the Unit had ceased operating on 14 February and had reverted to care and maintenance. Jennings Warehouse was cleared of all reminders of nearly eighteen years of RAF occupation by 23 March 1959.

CHAPTER SEVEN

THE DUTCH

On May 13, 1940, a telephone call from the Dutch Queen Wilhelmina woke King George VI from his sleep at 5 a.m, alerting him to the danger she was facing of being kidnapped and held as a hostage by the advancing German Army. Later that day she left The Hague and boarded the Royal Navy destroyer "Hereward" and crossed the North Sea to Harwich, from where she travelled to London and was met by the King. On May 14 Rotterdam was attacked by air and many civilians were killed. A large force of German airborne troops entered the City on the same day and at 9 a.m. on 15 May the Dutch capitulated and many soldiers were captured. However, about 1400 military personnel evaded capture and made their way to England.

The soldiers were first billeted in Haverfordwest but they were moved shortly afterwards to Dan-y-graig Camp, Porthcawl, where they were accommodated in tents. Of the 1460 who arrived, 120 were officers, 360 were senior NCOs and 980 corporals and privates. In the early days after their arrival they were guarded behind barbed wire by British troops because it was feared that there were fifth columnists amongst them. Their average age was 32, which was very high and many were in poor physique and were unfit for military duties.

The enduring recollection of the Dutch soldiers by those Porthcawl residents who lived in the town in 1940 is that they were all tall, good looking and wore the glamorous uniform of "Queen Wilhelmina's Bodyguard". The truth is that the soldiers were a mixture of the regular Dutch Army, the Marechaussee and the Politie Troepen. Sadly, there was no "Bodyguard", but the Marechaussee had the task in Holland of manning the borders and of providing general security throughout the country, including the responsibility for guarding the Royal Family. They wore impressive dark blue uniforms with white braiding and breeches tucked into high boots. The Politie Troepen were more or less police troops and wore grey-green uniforms, also with braiding. They did not retain their distinctive uniforms for long, however, as they were soon issued with standard British battledress uniforms.

Collectively they were known as the "Royal Dutch troops" (and also, as the

Piet Hoekman of the Dutch Marechausee. He was dropped in Holland in 1942 on a secret mission and captured. He was later killed. *Royal Marechausee Museum*

Dutch Legion) until 27 August 1941 when Queen Wilhelmina presented them with a standard in the name of the "Prinses Irene Brigade" and it is by this title that they are now officially remembered.

The 1460 men who had escaped from Holland were joined in Porthcawl by Dutchmen from America, Canada and South Africa and eventually they formed a brigade of a Headquarters unit, three companies with machine guns, mortars, anti-tank and light anti-aircraft guns, a reconnaissance squadron with armoured cars and an artillery battery. A replacement company was also formed from mariners who had been trained in America and whose duty it was to follow the Brigade in the field.

Mr L A K Wassen of Rotterdam, Holland was a soldier in the Dutch Infantry Brigade and was called up for "National Service" in October 1938. When Germany invaded Poland his unit was moved to the German/Belgian border, which was over-run when the Germans invaded Belgium and struck towards the French frontier. Mr Wassen escaped from the port of Brest in a Dutch ship, which landed him in what he believes was Cardiff, but was probably Plymouth. He remembers being given food and tea and then he was put on a train, eventually arriving at Dan-y-graig camp, Porthcawl. Mr Wassen was a cook who worked mainly in the Officer's Mess, which he has indicated was located in the area now occupied by the houses of Chestnut Drive. The camp gates were, he says, roughly where the concrete roadway of Dan-y-graig Avenue, which was built before the war, now joins with the tarmacadamed surface of the postwar housing development. Tents occupied the area up to the Porthcawl - Penybont boundary and the Marechaussee and Politie Troepen were accommodated towards the bottom of the slope, roughly in the area of Lime Tree Way. "I specially remember the first weeks in camp", Mr Wassen says. "We were not able to leave but after that period we went many times to Coney Beach and the pubs, where we started to learn English. The girls were wonderful teachers!"

The Dutch soldiers were very popular with the young ladies of the town - and also, it is said, with the jewellers, who are reputed to have rapidly exhausted their stocks as these were bought up as presents by the soldiers.

A Dutch Lieutenant who escaped from Brest in a Dutch ferry boat was Mr Jack de Waal, of Bussum, Holland. He landed in Plymouth and arrived in Porthcawl

Danygraig camp, July 1940.

Hans Sonnemans

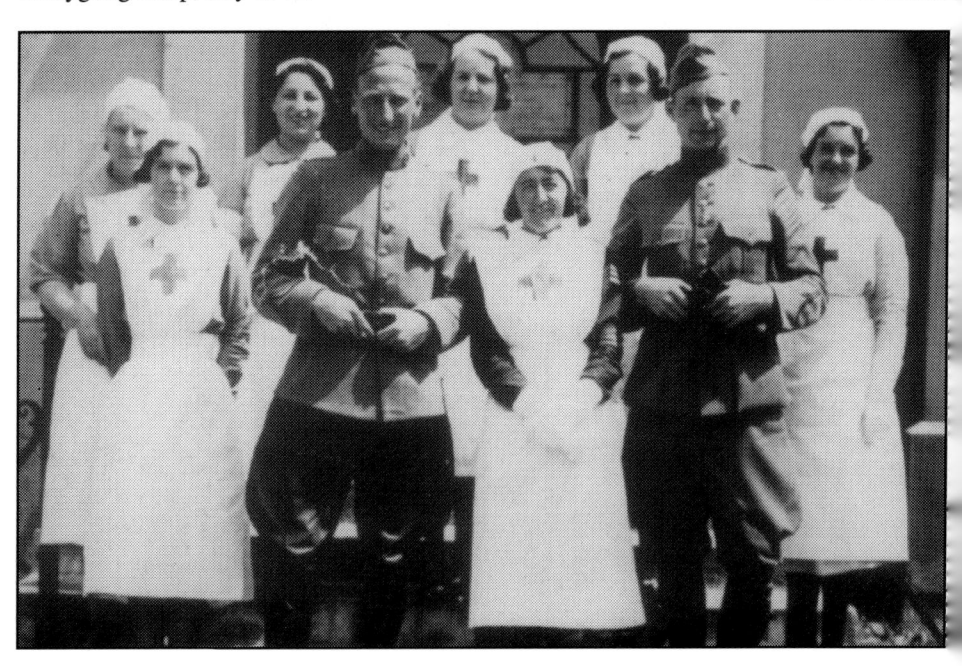

Sergeant H. Hertel (Right) with Sgt. Togt, Royal Dutch Army, outside Bridgend General Hospital.

H. Hertel

Dutch soldiers, in Danygraig camp, July 1940.   *Hans Sonnemans*

on 9 June 1940. Newton Church, the Seabank Hotel and the ice cream parlour owned by Mr R E Jones are vividly remembered. R.E. Jones Ltd owned the Marine Hotel and the Esplanade Hotel, including the adjoining ice-cream parlour (now a cafe) and a photograph of the Dutch Army parading outside their Headquarters in the Esplanade Hotel on the occasion of Queen Wihelmina'a Birthday, 31 August 1940 clearly shows "R.E. Jones Ltd" sign-written on the side of the Marine Hotel. Mr de Waal recalled that Mr Jones's daughter married a Dutch officer but says that she died some three years ago. Mr de Waal later married an English girl from Harrow, Middlesex, but during his stay in Porthcawl he made friends with several young ladies and still retains amongst his souvenirs an address scribbled on a piece of paper by a Peggy Lewis of South Place. Attempts to trace her have not been successful!

Lieutenant de Waal was sent with a platoon to guard the docks at Port Talbot and was there when Swansea was badly bombed. "I well remember the oil tanks burning and the sky dark with oily smoke and soot."

The first Dutch soldier in Porthcawl to be equipped with British battledress was Lt Col (retd) Hertel, of Eibergen. He was a Sergeant in the regular Dutch army when war broke out. His Dutch Army uniform had been badly damaged during the early part of the war and re-equipping him became an urgent necessity. Sergeant Hertel only spent three months in Porthcawl, before being transferred to London and becoming driver to Prince Bernard of the Netherlands.

The Dutch did not stay very long in Porthcawl. In September, 1940, the 2nd Battalion of the Dutch Legion, as it was then called, moved to Ruperra Castle, near Machen, which had been built in 1622 and rebuilt after a fire in 1789. King Charles 1 used as a refuge after the battle of Naseby in 1645. They were then moved to Conway, but shortly after they left the castle, it was badly damaged by fire, although the Dutch were not blamed! They later moved to a newly built camp at Wrottesley Park, just outside Wolverhampton and it was there, on 27 August 1941, that they became known as the Prinses Irene Brigade.

The Brigade trained with British units and on 6 August 1944 it embarked for Normandy and joined the British 6th Armoured Division east of the Orne, taking up a frontline position on 12 August and taking part in the advance towards the Seine. The Brigade was heavily involved in the fighting through Belgium and

Royal Dutch Army celebrates Queen Wilhelmina's birthday, August 31, 1940.

Queen Wilhelmina's Birthday Parade, August 31 1940, Dutch Anti-Aircraft Truck

Hans Sonnemans

Holland and on May 8, 1945 it entered The Hague as the first allied unit. The Brigade was disbanded at the end of 1945 but on April 15 1946 the Prinses Irene Regiment was established. It later became the Prinses Irene Guards Regiment and still maintains the traditions of the original Brigade that began in Porthcawl.

CHAPTER EIGHT

THE AMERICANS

On 7 December, 1941, the Japanese attacked the American Pacific Fleet at Pearl Harbour and this was followed by the declaration of war against the United States by Germany and Italy. The direct involvement of the Americans in the war that Britain had been fighting since 1939 was of immense significance and it eventually led to the defeat of the Axis forces.

Long before the Japanese attack, Winston Churchill and the American President, Franklin D. Roosevelt, had formed a strong relationship. From this had sprung Lease Lend (in December 1940), which enabled Britain to buy American ships and other equipment, with payment delayed until after the war. It also lead to the Atlantic Charter, signed on 19 August 1941, which spelt out the principles of freedom that were common to both the United States and the United Kingdom. Furthermore the President subsequently broadcast to the American people and spoke of the "final destruction of Nazi tyranny", which was regarded as highly controversial, coming as it did from a country that was not then at war with Germany.

In July 1941, five months before the United States entered the war, the British had drawn up a plan for an invasion of continental Europe "On the assumption that the USA is a belligerent".

When the United States entered the war there was a very strong lobby in that country pressing for the main military effort to be directed against Japan and it required all of Churchill's persuasive powers to convince the President that Germany must be dealt with first. Having accepted this, the Americans wanted an early invasion and pressed for an assault in the area of Boulogne and Le Havre as early as 1 April 1943. The British military recognised the impracticability of assembling an invasion force in such a short period and it was finally agreed that the invasion would take place on 1 May 1944 and a codeword, "Overlord", was given to the operation. In the event, the actual date of the invasion of Europe was 6 June 1944.

By mid 1943 there were some 238,000 U.S. troops in the United Kingdom, main-

Fred De Mary, U.S. 418th Engineers, with Cosy Corner Ballroom entrance behind in early 1944.

Carl V. Moore, U.S. 107th Field Artillery, on Porthcawl Pier.

ly in Northern Ireland. By D-Day this number had grown to 1 1/2 million, the vast majority of them in England and in South Wales. Many hundreds of these were stationed in Porthcawl.

The first American to report to the Porthcawl Garrison Engineer's Office, at "Brynteg", Green Avenue, did so on 24 July 1943. On 17 October, 1943 the 107th Field Artillery Battalion, which was part of the U.S. 28th Infantry Division, landed at Avonmouth Docks and was transported by road to Porthcawl on 18th October. The Battalion was accommodated in the Esplanade Hotel and in houses in Mary Street. The unit's Headquarters was in the "Riviera", a building now converted into flats next to the Marine Hotel. Carl V. Moore, formerly a staff sergeant with the 107th, who now lives in Beltsville, Maryland, recalls that he was accommodated in Room 310 in the Esplanade Hotel and still has a green mustard jar that he "filched" from the dining room, scratched the room number on it with a knife and sent home to his wife. He made friends with Mr. Cynwyd Beynon, whose family owned the town's two cinemas, the Casino and Coliseum and he remembers being entertained by Mr and Mrs Beynon in their apartment over one of the cinemas and being taken to clubs in Maesteg and to the British Legion Club (now the United Services).

"The only thing available was something called "fish and chips"", Mr Moore recalled "which were deep fried and wrapped in newspaper, sprinkled with vinegar. The potatoes were put in the bottom and a piece of fish on top. Beers at that time were primarily 'ale' and not refrigerated. Often the beer was in a large barrel which was kept on top of the bar and drawn by gravity from the bottom of the barrel".

"We parked our trucks, artillery pieces, graders, rollers, shovels etc on the Salt Lake motor pool area. I remember English lorries that were propelled by steam. They had hard rubber tyres and a boiler that sat just back of the cab and was fired to make steam to propel the load. Gasoline was at a premium during the war".

The battalion consisted of men from every State in the Union; men like "Hardrock" Harrigan, a tunnel worker from New York City, Lloyd Moe, from Hope, Idaho; Paul Betsill from Spartenburg, South Carolina, Carl Moore from Beltsville, Michigan and a Red Indian from Oklahoma. There were three artillery battalions in the 28th Division, the 107th, 108th and 109th and the 107th was called "Howitzers" or "Short Shots", its 105 mm howitzers giving light artillery support to the Infantry Battalions. "The Battalion consisted of five Batteries", explained former Staff Sergeant Carl V Moore. "Headquarters (admin and special tactics), A, B, and C with three guns each, firing semi-fixed shells with powder charges. There were seven alternatives charges that could be used, depending upon the distance needed to reach the target".

The 107th spent the first few weeks removing the thick rust-preventative grease which, before leaving the United States, had been daubed over their trucks, 105 mm artillery pieces, graders, trucks etc. The men were also exercised by forced marches of five, ten and finally twenty five mile stretches. Then, on 4th December, they were taken to the assault training centre at Braunton, near Woolacombe) in Devon for training. It was whilst they were at Braunton they suffered their first fatal casualty, when a corporal was killed. They returned to Porthcawl on 21 December and enjoyed a turkey dinner on Christmas Day. The Battalion moved out again on 5 January, 1944, for a five day exercise at Kittletop on the Gower peninsula, returning to Porthcawl on the 10th. An officer and eleven men of the Royal Artillery spent five days observing the Battalion's tactics and the Commanding Officer gave a farewell message to the men on 1 February in the Grand Pavilion, prior to his transfer to another unit. The Battalion spent from 14th to 22nd February at the Sennybridge firing range and was "outstanding among all other battalions".

On 27 March it was recorded that the Battery trained at Kenfig Burrows and that there was an Intelligence lecture on interrogating German prisoners in the Grand Pavilion and on 1 April, 1944, General (Ike) Eisenhower inspected the firing batteries of the unit at Newton Burrows.

Carl Moore remembered a particularly unpleasant form of training the troops endured in the technique of loading and unloading a troopship. A large container, some 40 ft high and about 30 ft square was built in the sea at Porthcawl. Cargo nets were let down on two sides and the soldiers, equipped with full field packs and rifles, were encouraged to climb to the top. When they got there they jumped "forced - maybe got a kick in the ass!" down into the water to be picked up and taken back to land. "This thing was there for a couple of weeks. I remember jumping off the top twice, then having to clean the equipment, including the rifle, before it rusted or became mildewed".

D-Day was fast approaching and orders came for the 107th to pack up and make the final move out of Porthcawl, leaving many grieving hearts behind. At 12.15 on 13 April the Battalion's trucks drove out of the Sale Lake motor park and headed for Tidworth where "the living quarters are by far the best that this organisation has occupied under its period of service". The Battalion was now part of the U.S. Third Army under General Patton. Training continued throughout the spring and early summer and on 21 July the men boarded their landing ships in Weymouth and landed at Omaha beach, after a rough crossing, on the following day.

The 107th Battalion, as part of the 28th Division, was involved in some of the fiercest fighting throughout the rest of the war. After landing it entered the "hedgerow" struggle north and west of St Lo, and, inching forward against desperate opposition, it took Percy on 1 August and Gathem on 10 August. The Commanding General, Brigadier General Wharton was killed on 12 August, only a few hours after assuming command. The Division reached and paraded through Paris on 29 August and continued fighting its way through France and Luxembourg to the German border and began hammering the Siegfried line on 12 September. The Division "smashed into the Hurtgen Forest on 2 November and in the savage seesaw battle that followed, Vossenack and Schmidt changed hands several times". The Battle of the Bulge, von Runstead's spectacular breakout at Bastogne in the Ardennes, began on 16 December and affected the entire front of the 28th Division. Every man including clerks and cooks, were used to hold up Von Runstead's advance, before withdrawing to Neufchateau for reorganisation. The Division, including the 107th battalion, had suffered heavy casualties and many soldiers had been captured by the advancing Germans. One of these was Technical Sergeant Harry Bryer, a 24 year old clerk in the Headquarters Office, who had become a close friend of a young Porthcawl girl, Doreen Anderson. Doreen, now Mrs Owen, worked in the booking office of Porthcawl Railway Station. "Harry was not a front line soldier", she remembers. "The Germans encircled the Headquarters staff at Wiltz in Luxemburg and captured them. They were marched back behind the German lines and given practically nothing to eat. From a diary he kept we know that he was living on grass soup and the weather was bitterly cold". T/Sgt Bryer died in German captivity.

The Division crossed the Rhine-Rhone Canal on 6 February and after one further attack towards the Ahr River, it was allocated training, rehabilitation and defen-

Tech Sgt. Harry Bryer, U.S. 107th Field Artillery Battalion, with Doreen Owen. He was later captured at Wiltz, Luxemburg in the Battle of the Bulge and died in captivity.

Doreen Owen

sive position responsibilities. It left France for the United States on 26 July 1945.

Although the 107th Field Artillery Battalion is believed to be the first American unit to enter Porthcawl, the records show that there were a considerable number of U.S. troops from a variety of units based in the town for varying periods of time.

On 22 October 1944 the S.S. "Brazil" left New York with 5000 troops of the 290th Regiment of the 75th Division, and joined a convoy across the Atlantic, arriving in Swansea on 1 November. They disembarked and were moved by train and motor transport to billets in and around Porthcawl. The Regiment's diary records that "Training and final preparations for combat kept men of the 290th occupied during the day but evening hours were spent in accordance with the individual's conscience. Dates with Welsh girls, dances arranged by Special Services and pleasant evenings of glasses of ale or stout seemed to be the more popular forms of relaxation. Restaurant dining proved interesting in that the menu occasionally featured tasty English delicacies and invariably offered the standard wartime fare of spam and chips".

One member of the 290th Regiment who well remembers his time in Porthcawl was Major (retired) Paul Ellis who was a Lieutenant with the 3rd Battalion. He was first accommodated in St. Donat's Castle and slept in "one of the most elaborate bedrooms I ever saw outside the movies" (possibly this was the bedroom formerly occupied by the American magazine multi-millionaire, Randolf Hearst or that of his mistress, film actress Marion Davies).
The Lieutenant was later outranked and forced to move to Porthcawl, where he was accommodated with five others at 32, Picton Avenue. He recalls that there was a coal pile about 50 feet high behind the house from which he took his weekly coal ration of 8lbs per person. "Nothing in my young life", says Mr Ellis, "had prepared me or any of us for what life was like in wartime Britain. The war had up until then been something of an inconvenience but not anything serious for those of us in the States to really worry about. Sure, we had rationing but it was no big deal. Most of us had never been more than 100 miles from home before and I don't know what we were expecting but we were surprised to find many of the houses, particularly in the larger towns, need painting and/or repairs. It took us a while to relate this to the fact that you had already been at war for more than four years".

Mr Ellis recalled that there was a small cafe owned by a young Greek where he and his fellow officers sometimes gathered. This was the "Victoria Cafe", which was at the corner of Victoria Avenue and South Road, opposite to the Rock public house, the premises of which are now the Bradford & Bingley Building Society and an amusement arcade. The cafe was owned by Paul, whose son now owns the mens' barber's shop in New Road. The cafe was very popular with American troops, who were always made welcome by Paul, who was from Cyprus, not Greece.

The 75th Division trained in the fields in and around Porthcawl and on one occasion 2nd Lieutenant Ellis was leading his platoon in a simulated attack on a barn, which was meant to represent a pill-box. The platoon was strung out in a ditch and the men were muddy, wet and cold and had been crawling around the fields for twenty-four hours. At this point two farmers were spotted watching the platoon's discomfort and displaying a great deal of hilarity. "I was very glad the men didn't have live ammunition" Mr Ellis grimly recalls.

On 24 November, 1944, the 5th Battalion of the 75th Division entertained all the under twelve year-olds in Porthcawl to a Thanksgiving Dinner in the Seabank Hotel. The children feasted on turkey, sweet potatoes, cranberry sauce and each was given a bag of fruit to take home.

The Division landed at le Havre and Rouen on 13 December and was almost immediately involved in the fierce fighting in the Ardennes, when it was rushed to the front to help stem Von Rundstedt's advance. It suffered heavy losses and casualties from the time it first engaged the enemy on 23 December along the Ourthe River and during its campaign which involved the capture of Vielsalm and Colmar, crossing the Rhine and relieving the British 6th Airborne Division near Roermond, in Holland. The Division continued to pursue the enemy, clearing the Haard Forest on 1 April, 1945 crossing the Dortmund-Ems Canal and clearing the approaches to Dortmund which fell to the 95th Division on 13 April. Its last battle was at Herdecke, which it captured on 13 April and it then moved to Brambauer for rest and recuperation, before being assigned security and military government duties in Westphalia.

There were many other American units in Porthcawl during those wartime years, and it has been possible to identify nearly all of them. The U.S. 342nd Engineers were camped at Plovers Plain, to the south of New Road, on what is now Trecco Bay Caravan camp. This was a flat area, protected by high sand-dunes. The Americans soon made friends with the locals and the school-children were regular visitors to the camp. Mr Dennis Purchase, who lives in New Road, still has his "My Buddy Book", which he bought at the Camp PX and filled in the details of the soldiers he had made friends with. "We used to rush home from school", he says, "and go over to the camp. The soldiers would give us money to get fish and chips for them".

One of the tasks of the Engineers was to construct bridges and many of Porthcawl's residents remember seeing these being built out from the end of Mackworth Road on to Coney Beach and from the Eastern Promenade. Roger E Athans, now living in St Petersburg, Florida, was with the 351st Engineers and was quartered in the Seabank Hotel. He remembers practising constructing Braithweight Pontoons and "camels feet" installations for docks and decking on the beaches at Newton. The 351st had a 15 piece dance band which played at the cinema/theatre at Cosy Corner, in the Pavilion, at Coney Beach, in the Esplanade and at the Seabank.

A reminder of the U.S. Engineers exists to this day at Hutchwyns Close, where at the base of what was once a sewer ventilation pipe can be seen impressed in the concrete the outline of a three turreted castle, the emblem of the Corps of U.S. Engineers. The U.S. Army Engineer Association says that "it is very common to find out Engineer branch insignia on projects completed by our soldiers" and also that "it was probably originally of metal and was removed by accident or on purpose". It was thought that there was a camp for U.S. soldiers surrounding Hutchwyns Close, and that a Nissen hut was provided cook house facilities. This is probably the only reminder of the U.S. military presence left in Porthcawl.

Another unit which was in the Porthcawl area from May 1944 was the 581st Engineers, but the men were quartered in Margam Castle. Alexander C Allen, of Jamesburg, New Jersey, remembers that the castle had its own hydro-electric generating system "and a hot house containing the only orange trees in your country". The 581st was a self-contained unit of 4 officers and 125 men and was equipped with 52 combination CMC trucks, two weapons carriers, two jeeps and one command car. When the unit sailed from Portsmouth for Utah beach on D-

"Castle" emblem of U.S. Engineers at Hutchwyns Close.

Day + 4 (June 10), it took with it a complete 1200 bed general hospital, fully equipped with everything except the staff. The unit was fortunate in that it did not lose a single soldier or any item of equipment during the subsequent fighting.

Fred De Mary, of Rivesville, West Virginia, was in the 418th Engineers Company, with a complement of 120 men and five officers. Their initial training began in March 1943, at Camp Claborne, Louisiana in March 1943 and on 11 August, 1943, the company travelled by train to Newport News Virginia, Port Norfolk. There they boarded the "Argentina" with 8500 troops and sailed to St John, Newfoundland and, after three days in port, they set across the Atlantic in a convoy of 16 ships. The crossing took sixteen days and the ship finally docked in Liverpool. The company embarked on a ferry boat ride up the Mersey and were amazed when the people of Liverpool lined the banks to cheer them. "It was a very warm welcome".

The 418th were transported to Porthcawl from Liverpool by train and stayed for about two weeks in the Seabank Hotel until their trucks arrived, when they moved to fields in the Bridgend area. "We lived in four-men tents and helped set up camping areas with other engineers. We built barracks for headquarters and put up tents for soldiers moving into our area. Part of the 28th Division was in our area" Mr De Mary has some good memories of his time in South Wales. "The people made us soldiers feel at home. We had a lot of tea parties and in the evening we would go dancing in the Grand Pavilion where the pretty girls taught us the hokey-cokey. We sure had a lot of fun!"

Towards the end of June 1944 the 418th moved firstly to Swanage, Dorset and then to Southampton, where they boarded a LST for Utah beach. They helped clear the port of Cherbourg, which had been badly damaged during the fighting after D-Day. Later the company moved to the Allied Headquarters at Valones, near Paris and during the Battle of the Bulge it transported reinforcement troops to Belgium.

On 28 December 1943 T/Sgt Joe Dzwonkowski boarded the S.S. "Argentina" in Boston, Mass., together with 20 officers, 326 construction specialists, including 18 divers, and 6 privates. they formed the 1053rd Port Construction & Repair Group and they landed at Gourock in Scotland on 8 January, 1944. They arrived in Porthcawl on 13 January and were initially accommodated in the Rest, before

Seabank Hotel - 1944. U.S. Soldiers on annexe roof.
Armed Guard at entrance.
Joe Dzwonkowski

1053 U.S. Engineers (Port Construction & Repair Group)
On parade outside Seabank Hotel, 1944.
Joe Dzwonkowski

moving to the Seabank on the 2 February. The unit was dispersed to towns all over the U.K., but T/Sgt Dzwonkowski, who was a dock and pile expert, remained in Porthcawl until 29 June, when he moved to Blandford, Dorset. The 1053rd regrouped prior to being shipped to "Utah" beach in Normandy on 15 August.

Joe Dzwonkowski remembers his stay in Porthcawl. "Most of the Welsh people were very nice. At the bar they would put out a bottle of whisky and on an afternoon off we would drink the bottle empty by the time the locals that were working came by. I don't think they appreciated us. At the time we seemed to have more money and we really spent it, which gave us a bad reputation, which we did not appreciate as we were not sure when or if we would come back".

Battery C, 113 AAA Gun Battalion, which was a unit of the American 1st Army and was employed in the defence of the 9th Army Air Corps, saw active service in North Africa with the British 8th Army. It was scheduled to take part in the Anzio landing in Italy but in July 1944 it was despatched from Algiers to Britain on HMS "Orion" with a contingent of Italian Army prisoners. "C" Battery, together with three others, guarded the prisoners and manned the Anti-Aircraft guns and enjoyed a rich menu provided by the Royal Navy, which included unsugared oatmeal and kippers for breakfast, bully beef for lunch and more kippers for dinner. On August 10 the ship docked in Gourock, Scotland and the men were transported by coach to Leek, Staffordshire. The camp was disliked from the start but the last straw was when the men were told that they would have to cut the grass with bayonets! A move was arranged to Davenport, near Wolverhampton, which was appropriately re-named "Wolf Town" by the servicemen, who received a warm reception from the locals. The Battery's task at Devonport was to clean up deserted camps, taking down tents and handing them in to the supply depot. When their work there was completed, the Battery moved by train to Porthcawl, arriving on 9 September 1944.

"We were stationed in the Seabank Hotel, probably the best hotel in Wales" the Battery's history records. "The girls were very friendly, maybe because we were the only G.I.'s in town. We worked every day cleaning up the hotels in town which had been occupied by the invasion forces. As we rode down the streets in British lorries, each man would take his position along the inside wall of the truck and with brooms and mops would simulate rowing, with 'coxwains' Marty Dorn

Sergeant Diefe Record & other members of Battery C, 113AAA Gun Battalion play "football" on the Green, West Drive, 1944.

Bernard La Duke

Bernard La Duke (on left) & Bob Mitchell, 'C' Battery AAA Gun Battalion outside "Louie's", now the Sportsmen Club, in 1944

and Bob Galagan calling the strokes. The people thought we were battle shocked veterans and we didn't try to tell them anything different!"

Bernard L LaDuke was a member of "C" Battery and was accommodated with five others on the second floor of the Seabank, facing the Bristol Channel. He was photographed outside "Louie's" on the Esplanade. During the war this was an ice-cream parlour owned by Louie Overington, whose husband, Jack, loved messing about in a boat and spent much of his time out at sea, fishing. Upstairs was a restaurant. One of the surprises encountered by first-time customers on the ground floor was that a very large Great Dane would to wander around the tables and as the seated customers were lower than the Great Dane's head, this could be an unnerving experience. "Louie's" is now the "Sportsmen's Club".

Mr LaDuke and "C" Battery were involved in the dramatic events of the 15 September 1944, which are related in the account of the Air Sea Rescue unit. A U.S. Steamtug had run aground on Tusker Rock in a storm and a U.S. motor towing launch, MTL 660, went to her assistance. The launch was swept ashore at Trecco Bay after its engine failed and "C" Battery was called upon to help.

"It was one heck of a night to go swimming", said Mr LaDuke. "We pulled it up on to the sands and there was a lot of big surf for such a nice bay. As a reward for rescuing the boat we were allowed to stand guard over it!"

As the unit's stay in Porthcawl came to a close, a dance was held in the Esplanade Hotel. "There was no lack of women and Don Pepley and Captain Julson led the Conga. Everybody had a good time".

On 12 November 1944 "C" Battery left Porthcawl by train and travelled to Leek and from there to Southampton. No transport had been provided and the men were obliged to march half a mile through pouring rain with their full kit and kit-bags. The following day they marched to the pier to join their ship which was to take them to Omaha Beach in Normandy. The ship turned out to be a former fish barge and the memory of its former occupation lingered strongly below decks!" "It's only for eight hours", the men were told but five days later they were still chugging miserably around the English Channel. The unit landed on D-Day + 138 and marched and bivouaced through the rain and mud to St Mere Eglise and from there to a spot close to Port de Lilas, which became the unit's favoured watering hole, nearby Paris proving to be too expensive, even for American servicemen. The Battery relieved the 143rd AAA at Liege in Belgium and was heavily involved in the Battle of the Bulge in December 1944.

It would appear that "C" Battery was the last U.S. Army unit of any size to be in Porthcawl and there were many in the town who missed the high spirited Americans. The effect of the friendly invasion on a small town by such large numbers of American servicemen is difficult to comprehend now, but in 1943, when the first U.S. troops arrived, Britain had suffered nearly four years of austerity, rationing and blackouts. Most of Porthcawl's young, fit men were in North Africa or Italy or were, at the very least, in camp at the other end of the country. Very few people had been to America and awareness of that country was confined to the glamourised picture conjured up by Hollywood. When the Americans arrived, their easy-going, friendly and courteous manner, together with their gifts of nylons, their well tailored uniforms, the soft material from which they were made contrasting so strongly with the "woolly blanket" texture of British uniforms, made them extremely popular, particularly with the young women of the town.

In compiling this record of the American occupation of Porthcawl in 1943 - 1944 I have heard from many ex-U.S. servicemen who were teenagers or were in their early twenties when they arrived in Porthcawl and who have referred to the warmth of the friendship that was offered to them by the townspeople. "The people of South Wales made us soldiers feel at home" is, perhaps, the most typical of the memories these veterans still retain of Porthcawl and there is no doubt that the American servicemen are still fondly remembered by many of the townspeople that I have spoken to.

Although some Americans undoubtedly used the "Hollywood illusion" to impress their girl friends, and spoke in expansive terms of the ranches or skyscrapers that they claimed they lived in back home, most U.S. servicemen were only too happy just to accept the friendship of the townspeople. Most of them had never travelled out of their home state before and were very homesick. There was always the sickening awareness that before they could return home they, the British and other Allied troops had to defeat the Germans who were massed along the French coast and that many would not make it. The relationships that developed between the British civilians and the American servicemen were often strong and long-lasting. Many local girls married G.I.'s and emigrated to the United States after the war. Many of the townspeople corresponded with American servicemen for several years after the soldiers returned home. "When the G.I.s left the fun went out of Porthcawl" is a view that is probably shared by many of those who were young in 1944.

INDEX

A
Air Sea Rescue 73-82, 106
Air Transport Auxiliary 3, 19
Air Training Corps 8, 18, 61
Allen, Alexander 100
Ambler, F/Sgt 76
Ambulance 10, 11
Americans 92-108
"Argentina", S.S. 102
Arnold, Geoff 54
Ash, G.E., LAC 77
Ashman, W/Cdr 66
Ashton, F.C., Major 25
Athans, R.E., 100

B
Baker, Ken 36
Bass, Sgt 25
Battle, LAC 60
Bevan, Evans 25
Beynon, Cynwyd 94
Beynon, William 4
Bluczynski, Sgt 61
Bond, LAC 59
"Brazil" S.S. 98
Bridgend 4, 10, 22, 26, 68, 70, 102
British Legion 6, 94
British Restaurant 13
Brogden, James 1
Brogden, Lucy 1
Bryer, Harry T/Sgt 96, 97
Burmester, R. Cmdr 73
Burnell, Cllr 17
"Brynteg" 94
Burnett, Sir C.S. 47

C
Carr, Ken 42
Cartwright, Cpt 25
"Casino" 4, 9, 14, 94
"Cato", S.S. 44
Chalke, Dr. 3, 6, 17
Chamber of Trade 12
Chivenor, RAF 82
Clarke, Ben H. 23, 25
"Clock Shop" 13
Coastguard 75, 77, 81
Cobham, Alan 19
"Coliseum" 4, 94
Coney Beach 25, 29, 42, 57, 79, 100
Cooper, Walter 2
Courtenay, William 8

D
Dan-y-graig Camp 26, 37, 43, 83, 85-87
David, Evan 10
David, John 14, 54, 55
David, John 10
Davies, T.A. 43
Davies, Telford 23
Davis, F/Sgt 65
Dawe, Mark 29
Dawson, W.J., Sgt 60
Deans, F/Sgt 65
Deere, David 9
Deere, R.P.T. 9
De Mary, Fred 93, 102
Denton, J.B. Sgt 60
Dindorf, Sgt 57
Dunkirk 4, 38
Dutch Army 26, 38, 83-91
Dzwonkowski, Joe 102

E
Eisenhower, "Ike", Gen 95
Elcock, Reg 29
Elliott, AC2 57
Ellis, Paul 98, 99
Esplanade 4, 6, 38, 70
Esplanade Hotel 41, 42, 88, 100
Evans, Colonel 25

F
Fire Service 2, 9, 79
Firstbrook, Captain 25
Flynn, Mike 75, 76
Franklyn, A.W., Gp. Captain 57
Francis F/Sgt 59
Free French 18, 21, 42, 50, 66-71

G
Gardner P/O 57, 59
Gendle A/C 76
"General Picton" 44
"Glamorgan Gazette" 4, 42
Gliding 65, 71
"Grand Pavilion" 1, 2, 6, 8, 13, 14, 17, 19, 21, 29, 42, 69, 72, 95, 100
Griffin Park 14, 18
Grisenthwaite AC2 65
Guiness 44

H
Hamill, K.W. 10
Hanbury, "Arty" 29
Hardesty, B.J., Sgt 60, 61
Hardy Edwin 29
Harries, Towyn 8
Hearst, Randolph 98
Hertel, H. 88
Hoare F/Sgt 60

Hocknell A/C	61	
Hoekman, Piet	84	
Holland AC2	65	
Homfrey, Colonel	29	
Home Guard	9, 18, 23-30	
Hutchwns Close	60, 100, 101	

I

Island Farm P.O.W. Camp	68

J

Jennings Warehouse	61, 73, 77, 82
Jenkins, Conway	2
Jenkins, D.	25
John, "Spadge"	29
John Street	11
Johnson, Amy	3, 19
"Jolly Sailor"	4
Jones, Arthur	29
Jones, Charles E.	29
Jones, David Walford	8
Jones, Ira "Taffy"	50, 54
Jones, J. Barry	29
Jones, Sir Thomas G.	13
Jones, Rev Vernon	37
Joseph, Morgan	25, 26, 29

K

Kelman, AC2	65
Kenfig	42, 57, 95
Keylock, Byron	54, 55
King George VI	30, 83
Kirkham, RAF	57
Kitching, P/O	59
Knoppik, Walter U/O	62
Knowles, AC2	65

L

LaDuke, Bernard	106
Lang, Walter	35
Lemon, J.N., F/O	54
Lewis, Councillor J.T.	1
Lewis, Peggy	88
Lewis, Peter	10
Llandow RAF	38, 65, 66
Llewellyn, Col. H.M.	25
Local Defence Volunteers	23-26
Lock, Jim	3, 6
"Lo-Cost"	4
"Louie's"	106

M

Marechaussee	83, 85
Marine Hotel	88, 94
McKewan, Lee	25
"Meals on Wheels"	4
Merthyr Mawr	29
Mollinson, Jim	19
4th Mon. Btn	43-46
Moon, Madeline, Cllr	i, 39
Moore, Carl V	93-95
Moxham, W/Cdr	66
Mumbles Lifeboat	79

N

Naylor, Sgt	59
Nelson AC1	60
Newton	2, 9, 13, 18, 19 29, 62, 88
Newton Burrows	26
Newton Down	47
Nottage	2, 14, 25, 26, 29, 38
Nottage Cemetery	62, 63 65

O

"Ocean View"	6, 43
Oliver, Bill Sgt	25
"Orion" HMS	104

Overington, Louie	106
Overington, Jack	106
Owen, Doreen	96, 97

P

"Paul the Greek"	99
Picton Avenue	25, 26
"Pier" Hotel	25
Pine, George Stanley	19-21
Plovers Plain	100
Police Station	23
Politie Troepen	83, 85
Porthcawl Council	1-4, 6 8, 9, 10, 11, 13 14, 17, 18, 21, 69
Porthcawl Museum	17, 19
Porthcawl Operatic Society	13
Porthcawl Senior School	14
Price, Peter P/O	10
Prinses Irene Brigade	83-91
Pritchard, H. Cdr.	14, 75
Puklo P/O	57
Purchase, Dennis	100

Q

"Queen Wilhelmina's Bodyguard"	83

R

Read, P/O	60
Reader, Ralph	67
Red Cross	1, 6, 17, 18
Reed, LAC	65
Rees, Ray	29, 78
Rest Bay	29, 54
Rest Home	6, 43, 44, 102
Richardson, A/C	57
Robinson, AC2	65
"Rock" Public House	25

Roffey, Sgt	60
Rogers, F.	25
Routledge, Sgt	63
Royal Army Service Corps	17, 18
Royal Artillery	18, 95
Royal Dutch Troops	83
Royal Observer Corps	11, 18, 31-36
Ruddell J. F/Sgt.	63

S

Salt Lake	94, 96
"Salute the Soldier Week"	16
"Sandpiper"	13
Saunders, Joe	25
"Seabank" Hotel	23, 25, 40, 41, 50, 60, 88, 99, 100, 103
Shackel, D. LAC	77, 79
Shepherd AC	57
Shimmans RSM	44
Shoesmith AC2	65
Shrimpton F/Sgt	62
Slingo, Lydia Pvt.	60
Smith, C.P.S. F/O	54
Smith, Deg	21
South Wales Borderers	23, 43, 46
S.S. "Stalheim"	73
St. Athan, RAF	3, 38, 71
St. Clare's Convent	12
St. Donat's Castle	98
St. John's School	10
Staunch A/C	57
Stoneleigh	4, 14, 23
Stormy Down, RAF	1, 4
21, 26, 45, 47-73, 75, 77	
Stratford, L.D. LAC	54
Strycharek Sgt.	63
Sullivan, AC2	59
Swann, F/Lt	59
Swansea	*2, 50, 81, 88, 98*

T

Tarling R. A/C	63
Taylor, Eva W. Cpl	60
Teskey Sgt.	62
Thomas, Glyndwr	17
Thomas, AC1	60
Thomas, Duncan Cpt.	25
Thomas, Ivor	29
Thomas, Oswald	18
"Thursday at Seven" Concerts	18
Thornewill, J.N. F/O	54
Thorndike, Dame Sybil	8
Tock, Sgt.	57
"Tournai", Nottage	29
Trecco Bay	79, 100

U

U.S. Launch MTL660	77, 78, 79, 106
U.S. Launch MTL816	79
U.S. Salvage Tug "Robert Emery"	79
U.S. Steamtug 672	77, 79
U.S. Units:	
5th Battalion, 290 Regt (75th Division)	98, 99
107th Field Artillery Btn (28th Div)	63, 94-108
113 AAA Gun Btn	104-106
342 Engineers	100
351 Engineers	100
418 Engineers	102
581 Engineers	100
1053 Port Construction Gp.	102

V

V.E. Day	*18, 69*
"Victoria Cafe"	99
V.J. Day	21

W

Waal de, Jack	85, 88
Wade, Sir Ruthven	50
Walker, Colin	44
"Warship Week"	14
"War Weapons Week"	9
Wardens, A.R.P.	2, 11
Wassen, L.A.K.	85
"Welcome Home Troops" Fund	17, 18
Welch Regiment	37-39
Westhorpe, A/C	77
Westmorland, F/Sgt.	65
West Riding Reconnaissance Regt.	39-41
West Yorkshire Regiment	18, 21, 41-42, 70
White, W.E.	41, 42
Wilhelmina, Queen	83, 85, 88
Williams, AC2	57
Wilson, Linton Mrs.	6
Winchester, Jack	61, 72
"Wings for Victory Week"	14, 15, 62
Womens' Voluntary Service	6, 18, 71
Woolworths	6
Wornum, Nancy Mrs.	6